Leading an Inclusive School

Other books by Authors

Creating an Inclusive School, Second Edition

ASCD MEMBER BOOK

Many ASCD members received this book as a member benefit upon its initial release.

Learn more at: **www.ascd.org/memberbooks**

Leading an Inclusive School

Access and Success for *ALL* Students

Richard A. Villa
Jacqueline S. Thousand

Alexandria, VA USA

1703 N. Beauregard St. • Alexandria, VA 223111714 USA
Phone: 800-933-2723 or 703-578-9600 • Fax: 703-575-5400
Website: www.ascd.org • E-mail: member@ascd.org
Author guidelines: www.ascd.org/write

Deborah S. Delisle, *Executive Director;* Robert D. Clouse, *Managing Director, Digital Content & Publications;* Stefani Roth, *Publisher;* Genny Ostertag, *Director, Content Acquisitions;* Allison Scott, *Acquisitions Editor;* Julie Houtz, *Director, Book Editing & Production;* Joy Scott Ressler, *Editor;* Georgia Park, *Senior Graphic Designer;* Mike Kalyan, *Director, Production Services;* Keith Demmons, *Production Designer.*

PAPERBACK ISBN: 978-1-4166-2286-4 ASCD product #116022
PDF E-BOOK ISBN: 978-1-4166-2288-8; see Books in Print for other formats.

Quantity discounts are available: e-mail programteam@ascd.org or call 800-933-2723, ext. 5773, or 703-575-5773. For desk copies, go to www.ascd.org/deskcopy.

ASCD Member Book No. FY17-3 (Dec. 2016 P). ASCD Member Books mail to Premium (P), Select (S), and Institutional Plus (I+) member on this schedule: Jan, PSI+; Feb, P; Apr, PSI+; May, P; Jul, PSI+; Aug, P; Sep, PSI+; Nov, PSI+; Dec, P. For current details on membership, see www.ascd.org/membership.

Library of Congress Cataloging-in-Publication Data

Names: Villa, Richard A., 1952- editor. | Thousand, Jacqueline S., 1950- editor.
Title: Leading an inclusive school : access and success for all students / [edited by] Richard A. Villa and Jacqueline S. Thousand.
Description: Alexandria, Virginia, USA : ASCD, [2017] | Includes bibliographical references and index.
Identifiers: LCCN 2016034663 (print) | LCCN 2016045732 (ebook) | ISBN 9781416622864 (pbk.) | ISBN 9781416622888 (PDF)
Subjects: LCSH: Inclusive education. | Educational equalization. | Educational leadership--United States. | School management and organization--United States.
Classification: LCC LC1200 .L43 2017 (print) | LCC LC1200 (ebook) | DDC 371.9/0460973--dc23
LC record available at https://lccn.loc.gov/2016034663

25 24 23 22 21 20 19 18 17 1 2 3 4 5 6 7 8 9 10 11 12

Leading an Inclusive School

LETTER TO THE READER

In 1975, Congress passed the Education for All Handicapped Children Act (EAHCA, Public Law [P.L.] 94-142), which guaranteed for the first time that all students with disabilities would receive a free and appropriate public education (FAPE) and learn in the least restrictive environment (LRE). When reauthorized in 1990, the name of the law was changed to the Individuals with Disabilities Education Act (IDEA, P.L. 101-476), and in 2004 it was amended by the Individuals with Disabilities Education Improvement Act (IDEIA, P.L. 108-446). Over the past 40 years, the law has been codified and provided a solid foundation for advancements related to inclusive schooling.

Amendments to IDEA in 1997 and 2004 have greatly strengthened the presumption that the placement of first choice for students with disabilities should be in the general education classroom, where they most readily have access to the rigorous general education curriculum and to the same co-curricular options as their classmates. As a result, the percentage of students with disabilities educated within general education environments has increased steadily.

Further bolstering IDEA is the Every Student Succeeds Act (ESSA, P.L. 114-95), the 2015 reauthorization of the 1965 Elementary and Secondary Education Act (ESEA; P.L. 89-10). The ESSA allows states greater flexibility in administering student learning accountability systems than did the legislation it replaces—the 2001 No Child Left Behind Act (NCLB, P.L. 107-110)—but maintains ESEA's legacy as a civil rights law by

- ensuring that states and districts hold schools accountable for the progress of every student subgroup (e.g., students with disabilities);
- continuing to dedicate resources and supports so that students with disabilities, English learners, and vulnerable student subgroups (e.g., children of low-income, homeless, or migrant worker families) have equitable access to rigorous curriculum and quality educators; and
- requiring districts to use evidence-based, whole-school interventions in their lowest-performing schools and in schools where subgroups (e.g., English learners, students with individual education programs) persistently underperform.

In short, ESSA reflects an increased public expectation that schools foster and be held accountable for maintaining high educational standards, equal opportunities for learning, and academic excellence for all students.

Our main reason for writing this book is that, 40 years after IDEA first came into effect, many educators still do not understand it or how to implement it and its accompanying legislation. And although schools and districts across the country have been educating students with disabilities in inclusive settings for many years, there remain many that have a long way to go toward implementing the spirit and the letter of IDEA. Too often, families still have to fight to get their children into general education classrooms and inclusive settings. What's more, some educators erroneously believe they are implementing inclusive practices when in fact they are not offering their students the academic and social support and differentiation that they require to succeed.

Schoolwide supports for all students have evolved significantly since IDEA was first signed into law. Proactive Universal Design for Learning (UDL) approaches to lesson and unit planning are replacing after-the-fact adaptations for select students. Frameworks such as Multitiered System of Supports (MTSS), Response to Intervention (RTI), and Schoolwide Positive Behavior Support (SWPBS) systems are in place at more and more schools, and some are specifically called for by state departments of education.

Cross-disciplinary teaming and co-teaching are rapidly becoming standard practice for differentiating instruction by weaving the knowledge and skills of the "masters of content" (i.e., general educators) with those of the "masters of access" (i.e., special educators, English language development specialists, related service personnel, and other specialists). In the chapters that follow, we hope to illuminate the many components of a new emerging schoolhouse model of inclusive education.

It is our experience that people often find the prospect of change daunting and tend to assume that others with greater authority or knowledge than them must surely be responsible for leading the way. But why not assume instead that leadership takes many forms and can come in many sizes? Why not adopt the conceptualization of leadership that noted group-theory experts Johnson and Johnson (2009) have to offer? If we define leadership as any action that helps to accomplish a task or to build interpersonal relations among those working together, every one of us has the capacity to lead change toward more inclusive schooling.

We hope that you will find this book a valuable addition to your professional library and that it will assist you in leading to advance school cultures that welcome, value, empower, and support the success of every child.

References

Elementary and Secondary Education Act of 1965 (ESEA PL 89-10). Retrieved from https://www.gpo.gov/fdsys/pkg/STATUTE-79/pdf/STATUTE-79-Pg27.pdf.

Every Student Suceeds Act. (2015). *The 2015 reauthorization of the Elementary and Secondary Education Act* (PL 119-45). Retrieved from www.ed.gov/essa?src=rn.

Johnson, D. W., & Johnson, F. (2009). *Joining together: Group theory and group skills* (10th ed.). Boston: Allyn & Bacon.

No Child Left Behind. (2001). *The 2001 reauthorization of the Elementary and Secondary Education Act (HB1).* Retrieved from https://www.congress.gov/bill/107th-congress/house-bill/1.

SECTION I

Before launching into the *how* of creating an inclusive school, we offer here two chapters and one Voice of Inclusion to set the stage for the strategies presented in subsequent chapters.

Chapter 1 examines the *what* of inclusive education, providing both legal and pragmatic definitions of inclusive schooling, examining an inclusive 9th grade English language arts class in action, and connecting inclusive schooling to national school-restructuring initiatives. Chapter 2 examines the *why* of inclusive schools and offers 10 rationales for creating and maintaining them. Finally, "From My Friend, Ro Vargo" offers a family's perspective on inclusive education.

CHAPTER 1

An Inclusive School: Providing Access and Success for All

Mary A. Falvey and Christine C. Givner with Richard A. Villa and Jacqueline S. Thousand

There is only one child in the world and the child's name is ALL children.

—Carl Sandburg

An Inclusive Classroom in Action

What does an inclusive school look and sound like? The following scenario describes a freshman language arts class on a typical day in the life of 32 students attending an ordinary yet extraordinary high school in a large urban school district.

It is 3rd period in Mr. Rice's freshman English language arts class, and the 32 students have just finished "reading" the final chapter of *To Kill a Mockingbird* by Harper Lee (1960). Students have listened to the book using text-to-speech software, read versions of it written at lower readability levels, or read it in both English and their native language to accommodate their limited English literacy levels. All the students have either created or been given graphic organizers to help them organize key ideas. The students have been working on the California English Language Arts standards while reading the book. Although the students have diverse learning styles and abilities, all are challenged in meaningful ways that relate to the state standards. Mr. Rice has just assigned a culminating task for partners to creatively depict how the characters in *To Kill a Mockingbird* demonstrate courage and conviction. He also has distributed a rubric describing how the assignments will be evaluated.

Several students in Mr. Rice's class qualify for special education services, five qualify for gifted and talented services, and a quarter of them are bilingual in Spanish and English and considered long-term English language learners. Mr. Rice meets with a team weekly to support the differentiation of materials, instruction, and assessment for his students.

The coordinator of the gifted and talented support services, Ms. Stremel, has worked with Mr. Rice to develop a personal learning contract with the five students she serves to identify how each of them will not only meet but exceed the assignment rubric. Mr. Gonzales, the 9th and 10th grade English language development educator, is working with Mr. Rice to develop students' academic language in English and plan visual and other scaffolds to make content more accessible to English language learners. Mr. Gonzales co-teaches with Mr. Rice on Mondays, at which time he models the explicit academic language development strategies the two have planned to use for the week. Ms. Mikel, Mr. Rice's special education support teacher, co-teaches in the classroom Tuesday through Thursday and is available (as is Mr. Rice) to offer guidance and support not only to the students eligible for special education, but to any student who may want or need assistance.

Each of the long-term English language learners in the class is partnered with an English- and Spanish-speaking classmate who has a stronger grasp of English academic language. The pairs have a choice of preparing presentations in both English and Spanish that feature visual aids or preparing them in English only.

Jesus, one of Mr. Rice's students, qualifies for special education services because of a learning disability. He reads well below grade level, but has excellent verbal and visual/spatial skills. For this assignment, he is partnered with Emily, who is very skilled in reading and writing but struggles with oral reading skills. The two students use their complementary strengths to put together a presentation describing how the *To Kill a Mockingbird* characters demonstrate courage and conviction.

George, a student with autism, and Quon receive guidance from Mr. Rice in designing their presentation. George will show pictures of the characters with brief written descriptions that he and Quon have composed.

Casandra, who has multiple disabilities, uses a motorized chair to get around and an electronic communication device to convey her thoughts and responses. Her partner is Jimmy, who qualifies for gifted and talented services. Jimmy surfs the web for information related to the topic, and then he and Casandra decide what to include in their presentation. Casandra and Jimmy enter their content into Casandra's electronic device, which has a voice output that will be activated to deliver their presentation to the class.

Inclusive Education: Whose Responsibility Is It?

The composition of Mr. Rice's class reflects the increasing diversity in many classrooms throughout the United States. At one time, many of the students in such a class would have been labeled and forced into separate classes, thereby limiting their exposure to one another, the essential curriculum, and varied instructional methods and personnel. Some students would have been moved to a gifted and talented program. The students still developing academic English proficiency would have been left to sink or swim in a classroom with little explicit attention paid to academic language development, modification of language demands, visual supports, or natural peer support to help students make sense of learning. Jesus, Casandra, and George's eligibility for special education would have led them to be placed in segregated special education programs or "special education" language arts classes.

Some argue that the social justice occurring in Mr. Rich's class—inclusive education—is not the responsibility of schools. But if not, then whose responsibility is it? A country's systems and institutions teach by example what the country, state, or community values: either inclusion or segregation and exclusion. Inclusive education demands that schools create and provide whatever is necessary to ensure that all students have access to meaningful learning. It does not require students to possess any particular set of skills or abilities as a prerequisite to belonging in a "regular" classroom.

The Legal Definition of Inclusive Education

The legal mandate driving inclusive education in the United States originated in 1975 with the promulgation of Public Law (P.L.) 94-142, the Education for All Handicapped Children Act (EAHCA), which was reauthorized in 1990 as the Individuals with Disabilities Education Act (IDEA, P.L. 101-476) and amended by the Individuals with Disabilities Education Improvement Act (IDEIA, P.L. 108-446) in 2004. Although the specific terms *inclusion* and *inclusive education* are not found in the law, the law guarantees students with disabilities a *free and appropriate public education* (FAPE) in the *least restrictive environment* (LRE). Specifically, the law requires that each public agency (including school districts) ensure the following results:

> (i) To the maximum extent appropriate, children with disabilities, including children in public or private institutions or other care facilities, are educated with children who are not disabled; and
>
> (ii) Special classes, separate schooling, or other removal of children with disabilities from the regular educational environment occurs only when the nature or severity of the disability is such that education in regular classes with the use of supplementary aids and services cannot be achieved satisfactorily. (34 C.F.R. § 300.114 [A][2])

Every subsequent reauthorization of the original 1975 federal law has reaffirmed the preference of the U.S. Congress that children with disabilities be educated in general education classrooms with their similar-aged peers unless there is a compelling educational justification otherwise. The law requires that the LRE be determined based upon each individual student's strengths and needs by a team composed of people who have expertise and experience with the student, including parents and, whenever possible, the student herself. If the team determines that a student can progress toward meeting goals in general education with the use of supplementary aids and services, then general education is the LRE for that student.

The critical language used in the law is "with the use of supplementary aids and services." When EAHCA was first passed in 1975, the professional education literature offered scant information on strategies for using supplementary aids and services to effectively include students with disabilities. However, since that time, much has been learned and communicated on the matter (see, for example, Brown, McDonnell, & Snell, 2016; Janney & Snell, 2013; Shogren, McCart, Lyon, & Sailor, 2015; Thousand, Villa, & Nevin, 2015). In fact, attention has now shifted to methods for differentiating instruction for all students.

Since the promulgation of EAHCA, the LRE mandate and federal court decisions have built upon one another to clarify the following guidelines:

- School districts must consider general education placement for all students with disabilities, regardless of the degree of the disability.
- Academic and social benefits of general education placement must be taken into serious consideration.
- Students with disabilities should not merely be "dumped" into a general education setting; they must receive the necessary supports, services, and supplementary aids.

The standard for denying inclusive education to a student with disabilities is very high.

The Pragmatic Definition of Inclusive Education

So what does inclusive schooling look like in practice? To begin to answer that question, we have asked thousands of children, adolescents, and adults to identify two events in their lives: one that caused them to feel included and one that caused them to feel excluded. We also asked them to describe how they felt during and following the two experiences (see Figure 1.1 for a sampling of their responses).

Examining individuals' reactions to inclusion and exclusion is critical to any discussion of educating all students together in the same classrooms. Figure 1.1 makes the powerful point that no one wants to feel excluded. As Falvey, Givner, and Kimm describe in *Creating an Inclusive School* (1995),

> An inclusive school values its students, staff, faculty, and parents as a community of learners. An inclusive school views each child as gifted. An inclusive school cherishes and honors all kinds of diversity as an opportunity for learning about what makes us human. Inclusion focuses on how to support the special gifts and needs of each and every student in the school community to feel welcomed and secure. (p. 8)

FIGURE 1.1

Feeling Excluded vs. Feeling Included

Excluded	**Included**
Angry	Proud
Ashamed	Secure
Resentful	Special
Hurt	Comfortable
Frustrated	Recognized
Lonely	Confident
Different	Happy
Confused	Excited
Isolated	Trusted
Inferior	Cared about
Worthless	Liked
Invisible	Accepted
Substandard	Appreciated
Unwanted	Reinforced
Untrusted	Loved
Unaccepted	Grateful
Closed	Normal
	Open
	Positive

We define inclusive schooling as welcoming, valuing, empowering, and supporting the academic, social/emotional, and language and communication learning of all students in shared environments and experiences for the purpose of attaining the goals of education (Villa & Thousand, 2016). Inclusive schooling is making a commitment to provide each student in the community—each citizen in a democracy—with the inalienable right to belong and not to be excluded. Inclusion assumes that living and learning together benefits everyone, not just children who are labeled as having a difference (e.g., those who are considered gifted, are not yet English-proficient, or have a disability).

Inclusion is a value and a belief system, not just a set of strategies. Mr. Rice's language arts class is not just about accommodations, supports, and differentiated instruction; it also is about an attitude that is intentionally taught by example. Once adopted by a school or school district, an inclusive vision drives all decisions and actions by those who subscribe to it. People shift from asking first-generation inclusion questions (e.g., "Why inclusion?" "Does this child belong?") to asking second-generation questions (e.g., "What can our school do differently to successfully include all students?" "How might I differentiate my materials, instruction, and ways of assessing students so all students are participating and learning?").

Implications of Inclusive Education

As Figure 1.1 illustrates, exclusion of any sort can have devastating effects. It conveys a strong message to students that they do not measure up or fit in, stigmatizing them as an underclass. Exclusive or exclusionary thinking and practices can create a situation where belonging is something that needs to be earned rather than considered an unconditional human right. Norman Kunc (2000) speaks of the casualties of exclusion or "conditional acceptance," arguing convincingly that many of the current problems facing youth at risk (e.g., those who are in gangs, suicidal, or dropping out of school) are the consequences of an inflexible, insensitive education system that methodically (though unintentionally) destroys the self-esteem of students who do not "fit the mold." In a seminal work that describes the plight of youth at risk from an American Indian perspective, Brendtro, Brokenleg, and Van Bockern (2009) list *belonging* as one of the four central values that create a child's "Circle of Courage." The right to belong is *everyone's* birthright; given the increasing numbers of at-risk students in U.S. schools and the centrality of the need to belong, schools must work to reclaim youth who feel marginalized or excluded.

The growing diversity of the student population in U.S. schools is a topic of continued discussion and concern. Students may exhibit significant differences related to language, culture, religion, gender, abilities, sexual orientation, socioeconomic status, and geographic setting. Interestingly, these differences are often seen more as a problem than as offering an opportunity for learning about the rich variety of life and how we can include, value, respect, and welcome one another for who we are. In 1992, Grant Wiggins wrote the following about the value of diversity:

> We will not successfully restructure schools to be effective until we stop seeing diversity in students *as a problem*. Our challenge is not one of getting "special" students to better adjust to the usual schoolwork,

> the usual teacher pace, or the usual tests. The challenge of schooling remains what it has been since the modern era began two centuries ago: ensuring that *all* students receive their entitlement. They have the *right* to thought-provoking and enabling schoolwork, so that they might use their minds well and discover the joy therein to willingly push themselves farther. They have the *right* to instruction that obligates the teacher, like the doctor, to change tactics when progress fails to occur. They have the *right* to assessment that provides students and teachers with insight into real-world standards, useable feedback, the opportunity to self-assess, and the chance to have dialogue with, or even to challenge, the assessor—also a *right* in a democratic culture. Until such a time, we will have no insight into human potential. Until the challenge is met, schools will continue to reward the lucky or the already equipped and weed out the poor performers. (pp. xv–xvi)

Inclusive Education and School Restructuring

The call for restructuring the education system so that it offers high and meaningful educational standards, equitable learning opportunities for every student, and accountability from educators requires individual and collective commitment and hard work. At a minimum, any school restructuring effort requires educators to hold the following beliefs:

- Each student has strengths and needs.
- Each student can and will learn and succeed.
- Each student has unique contributions to offer other learners.
- Diversity enriches us all.
- Students can overcome risks of failure through involvement in a thoughtful and caring community of educators and learners.
- Effective learning results from the collaborative efforts of everyone working to ensure each student's success.
- Supports and services need to "fit" the student (i.e., they must be comprehensive, flexible, and personalized) rather than the student needing to "fit into" existing services.

Restructuring efforts in special education have parallel efforts in general education, as they intentionally raise fundamental questions regarding the most effective ways to educate all students. In the more than two decades since the publication of *Creating an Inclusive School* (1995), we are heartened to see that general and special education restructuring initiatives have converged and become aligned due to shared social justice objectives and increased accountability for the learning of all students. Together, these initiatives have yielded innovations and conceptualizations of unified standards and systems to facilitate student achievement and success. Nearly all states have adopted rigorous Common Core standards or other standards designed to ensure college- and career-readiness for every student. Schools have worked to align policy and practice so as to provide research-based instruction in general education and swift, targeted interventions (e.g., through the Positive Behavior Intervention and Supports and Multitiered System of Supports frameworks). Chapters 3–7 of this book detail school restructuring and instructional innovations that allow both inclusive education for students with disabilities and academic engagement for all.

Final Thoughts

An inclusive education orientation and a set of inclusive practices benefit not only students with disabilities, but *all* students, educators, parents, and community members. As communities and schools embrace the true meaning of inclusion, they become better able to transform special education into an inclusive service-delivery system and a society intolerant of difference into one that celebrates students' natural diversity with meaningful, student-centered learning.

Inclusion is not a programmatic set of special strategies, but rather a way of life that is based upon the belief that each individual is valuable and belongs. We invite you to experience a more personal view of inclusive education by reading the "Voice of Inclusion" that follows Chapter 2.

References

Brendtro, L. K., Brokenleg, M., & Van Bockern, S. (2009). *Reclaiming youth at risk: Our hope for the future* (Rev. ed.). Bloomington, IN: Solution Tree Press.

Brown, F., McDonnell, J., & Snell, M. E. (2016). *Instruction of students with severe disabilities* (8th ed.). Boston: Pearson.

Education for all Handicapped Children Act of 1975, PL 94-142, 20 U.S.C. 1400 et seq.

Falvey, M., Givner, C., & Kimm, C. (1995). What is an inclusive school? In R. Villa & J. Thousand (Eds.), *Creating an inclusive school* (pp. 1–12). Alexandria, VA: ASCD.

Harper, L. (1960). *To kill a mockingbird.* Philadelphia: Lippincott.

Individuals with Disabilities Education Act (IDEA) of 1990, PL 101-476, 20 U.S.C. 1400 et seq.

Individuals with Disabilities Education Improvement Act (IDEIA) of 2004, U.S.C. § 1400 et seq.

Janney, R., & Snell, M. S. (2013). *Modifying schoolwork* (3rd ed.). Baltimore: Paul H. Brookes.

Kunc, N. (2000). Rediscovering the right to belong. In R. A. Villa & J. S. Thousand (Eds.), *Restructuring for caring and effective education: Piecing the puzzle together* (2nd ed., pp. 77–92). Baltimore: Paul H. Brookes.

Office of Special Education and Rehabilitative Services. (2014). *36th annual report to Congress on the implementation of the Individuals with Disabilities Education Act.* Alexandria, VA: ED PUBS, Education Publications Center, U.S. Department of Education. Available: http://www2.ed.gov/about/reports/annual/osep/2014/parts-b-c/36th-idea-arc.pdf.

Shogren, K., McCart, A., Lyon, K., & Sailor, W. (2015). All means all: Building knowledge for inclusive schoolwide transformation. *Research and practice for persons with severe disabilities, 40*(3), 173–192.

Thousand, J. S., Villa, R. A., & Nevin, A. I. (2015). *Differentiating instruction: Planning for universal design and teaching for college and career readiness* (2nd ed.). Thousand Oaks, CA: Corwin Press.

Villa, R.A., & Thousand, J. S. (Eds.) (1995). *Creating an inclusive school.* Alexandria, VA: ASCD.

Villa, R. A., & Thousand, J. S. (2016). *The inclusion checklist: A self-assessment of quality practices.* Port Chester, NY: National Professional Resources.

Wiggins, G. (1992). Foreword. In R. A. Villa, J. S. Thousand, W. Stainback, & S. Stainback (Eds.), *Restructuring for a caring and effective education: An administrative guide to creating heterogeneous schools* (pp. xv–xvi). Baltimore: Paul H. Brookes.

CHAPTER 2

The Rationales for Creating and Maintaining Inclusive Schools

Richard A. Villa and Jacqueline S. Thousand

Consider the following question: *What do you believe the goals of education should be?* In other words, what are the outcomes, attitudes, dispositions, and skills you want the children you care about to possess by the time they exit high school? After you have answered this question from your own perspective, try answering it again from the perspective of others. Think of students both with and without disabilities. Think of adults whose roles differ from your own (e.g., parents, other educators, school board members, local businesspeople, community members). What do you notice? Do your responses have anything in common?

We've had the opportunity to pose the above question to tens of thousands of parents, teachers, administrators, students, university professors, and concerned citizens across the Americas, Europe, Asia, Africa, India, Australia, and the Middle East. Regardless of the respondents' divergent perspectives and vested interests, answers all tended to fall into one or more of the four categories shown in Figure 2.1.

Intriguingly, the four categories in Figure 2.1—belonging, mastery, independence, and generosity—are also the four main components of the "Circle of Courage" in traditional American Indian culture (the Lakota tribe, in particular) (Brendtro, Brokenleg, & Van Bockern, 2009). Judging from the uniformity of responses from people all over the world, a hunger exists for curriculum that reaches beyond traditional academic domains to address

FIGURE 2.1

Frequently Identified Goals of Education by Category

Belonging
- Having friends
- Forming and maintaining relationships
- Being part of a community
- Feeling good about oneself
- Getting along with others, including coworkers
- Being a caring parent and family member
- Being happy

Mastery
- Experiencing success and becoming competent in something or some things
- Being well rounded
- Being a good problem solver
- Being flexible
- Being motivated
- Having literacy, numeracy, technology, and communication competence
- Being a lifelong learner
- Reaching one's potential in areas of interest

Independence
- Having choice in work, recreation, leisure, or continued learning
- Possessing the confidence to take risks
- Being as independent as possible
- Assuming personal responsibility
- Holding oneself accountable for actions and decisions
- Being able to self-advocate
- Being adaptable and flexible

Generosity
- Being a contributing member of society
- Valuing diversity
- Being empathetic
- Offering compassion, caring, and support to others
- Being a responsible citizen
- Giving back to the community
- Exercising global stewardship

concerns such as those so poignantly expressed in the famous letter to teachers from a Holocaust survivor (see Figure 2.2).

Historically, "special education" practices have unintentionally interfered with students' opportunities to experience the four components of the Circle of Courage. In a misguided effort to foster their skills development and independence, we have relegated our students with special

FIGURE 2.2

Letter to Teachers from a Holocaust Survivor

Dear Teachers,

I am a survivor of a concentration camp. My eyes saw what no man should ever witness: gas chambers built by learned engineers; children poisoned by educated physicians; infants killed by trained nurses; woman and babies shot and burned by high school and college graduates. So I am suspicious of education.

My request is: Help your students become human. Your efforts must never produce learned monsters, skilled psychopaths, educated Eichmanns. Reading, writing, and arithmetic are important only if they serve to make our children more human.

Source: Adapted from *Teacher and Child* by H. Ginott, 1972, New York: Macmillan. Reprinted with permission.

needs to environments separate from the general student body. Although it is important for students to develop skills, it is difficult for them to feel that they belong when they are sent down the hall or to a different school from their peers. Practically every theory of motivation stresses the importance of fulfilling children's need to belong (see Brendtro, Brokenleg, & Van Bockern, 2009; Glasser, 1986; Maslow, 1970). When we exclude or remove a child from the general education environment, we are tacitly instructing them that belonging is a privilege that must be earned. Norman Kunc (2000) describes the dilemma:

> The tragic irony . . . is that as soon as we take away students' sense of belonging, we completely undermine their capacity to learn the skills that will enable them to belong. Herein lies the most painful "Catch-22" situation that confronts students with disabilities—they can't belong until they learn, but they can't learn because they are prevented from belonging. (p. 88)

When we closely examine the goals of education and acknowledge both that they extend beyond academics and that they are the same for all children, the next logical step is to question why we would continue to countenance a divided educational system that produces dire consequences for so many children.

Changing Assumptions

Most people we've asked have told us that they don't think the fundamental organization of most schools has changed much over the decades. At the same time, few would deny that the world is now dramatically different from the way it was in the days before social media and the information explosion in which we find ourselves today. The rapid proliferation of new technological discoveries, cooperative international businesses, and societal trends, combined with an exponential growth in available knowledge, makes it impossible for us to keep abreast of all there is to know. Meanwhile, our educational system is still organized as it was when the animating goals were to prepare workers for farm and factory labor, to sort out the elite for continuing education, and to assimilate new immigrants into a predominantly Protestant and Anglo-Saxon culture.

Schooling must now be based on the assumption that modern society is globally interconnected, multicultural, and multilingual. To succeed in such a society, educators and employers alike encourage developing such traits as strong communication skills, creative problem-solving abilities, interpersonal skills, the ability to cope with adversity and uncertainty, and a willingness to engage diverse perspectives. The heart of the 21st century curriculum lies in learning both how to learn and how to maintain a lifelong passion for inquiry.

Delivery of a new curriculum that more fully meets students' present-day needs requires trying new strategies, including—but hardly limited to—cooperative group learning, differentiated instruction, active student-directed learning, detracking, focusing on social and communication skills, and community service. When we assume student diversity rather than homogeneity, we can accelerate the transformation of our schools and better prepare every student for future success.

Efficacy Data

Question: What is the most prominent way of assessing student performance in the United States?

Answer: Norm-referenced standardized achievement tests.

Question: If we agree with the tens of thousands of people who identify the development of skills related to belonging, mastery, independence, generosity, communication, and inquiry as important goals of education, what standardized achievement tests can we use to assess student performance in these areas?

Answer: None.

In education, we do not always measure what we say we value or consider critical for our children's success. What, then, *do* we measure for students receiving special education services, and what are the results of these measures?

As early as the 1980s, research reviews and efficacy studies have measured the global school performance of students who receive special education services. Early studies showed that separate special education services had little to no positive effects on students regardless of the intensity or type of their disabilities. Subsequent large-scale studies yielded even worse results: In a 1994 review of three meta-analyses of effective special education settings, Baker, Wang, and Walberg concluded that "special-needs students educated in regular classes do better academically and socially than comparable students in non-inclusive settings" (p. 34). Their findings held true regardless of the student's grade level or type of disability. In their 2000 review of 36 studies of children with intellectual disabilities, Freeman and Alkin came to exactly the same conclusion. A study of 11,000 students with disabilities by Blackorby and colleagues (2005) found that students who spent more time in general education than their peers performed closer to grade level, had higher test scores, and were less frequently absent.

According to the U.S. Department of Education, "across a number of analyses of post-school results, the message was the same: those who spent more time in regular education experienced better results after high school" (1995, p. 87). Researchers have also found that the inclusion of students with even significant support needs does *not* have adverse effects on their classmates' academic success (Hollowood, Salisbury, Rainforth, & Palombaro, 1995; Sharpe, York, & Knight, 1994). In fact, Kalambouga, Farrell, and Dyson (2007) found that the inclusion of students with disabilities has, for the large part, either neutral or positive effects on the rest of the students. Inclusion of students with significant support needs has actually been shown to enhance academic achievement and self-esteem and diminish abstenteeism for all students (see Cole & Meyer, 1991; Costello, 1991; Kelly, 1992; Strain, 1983; Straub & Peck, 1994).

Finally, it is important to note that there are racist and classist aspects to the continued segregation of special education programs in schools. It is well established that English language learners, students from low-income families, and students of color (especially those who are black, Latino, or American Indian) are grossly and persistently overrepresented in special education classes (Rebora, 2011).

Legal Issues

Overall, the data speak volumes. As the Individuals with Disabilities Education Improvement Act acknowledges, "over 30 years of research and experience has demonstrated that the education of children with disabilities can be made more effective by having high expectations and ensuring students' access in the general education curriculum to the maximum extent possible . . . [and] providing appropriate special education and related services and aides and supports in the regular classroom to such children, whenever possible" (20 U.S.C. § 1400 [c][5]).

Since 1975, federal law has consistently reflected Congress' preference for educating children with disabilities in general education classrooms. In that time, circuit and federal court rulings have further clarified the intent of the law:

- Roncker v. Walter (1983) addressed the issue of "bringing educational services to the child" versus "bringing the child to the services." The case was resolved in favor of inclusion and established the principle of portability: namely, that "if a desirable service currently provided in a segregated setting can feasibly be delivered in an integrated setting, it would be inappropriate under P.L. 94-142 [IDEA] to provide the service in a segregated environment" (700 F.2d at 1063).

- In 1989, the U.S. Court of Appeals ruled in favor of Timothy W., a student considered "too disabled" to be entitled to an education by his school district. The ruling clarified the responsibility of school districts to educate all children and specified that the term "*all*" used in IDEA meant to include every child with disabilities, regardless of severity (1989).
- In Oberti v. Board of Education (1993), the Third Circuit Court of Appeals upheld the right of Rafael Oberti, a boy with Down syndrome, to receive his education in his neighborhood school with necessary supports, placing the burden of proof for complying with IDEA's LRE requirements squarely on the school district and state rather than the family.
- In 1994, the Ninth Circuit Court of Appeals upheld a district court's decision in Sacramento Unified School District v. Holland that school districts must always consider the general education environment first when placing students with disabilities.
- In 2002, the Third Circuit Court of Appeals upheld a district court's decision in Girty v. School District of Valley Grove to keep Charles "Spike" Girty, a student with moderate disabilities, in the general education environment. The appeals court rejected the school district's contention that Spike needed to be segregated because his educational level was significantly below that of his classmates, noting the following:

> IDEA requires only that Spike be able to receive educational benefits when he is in the regular class, and that the benefits he receives when in the regular class with supplementary aids and services not be far outweighed by the benefits he would receive in a self-contained segregated setting. . . . States and school districts are not asked to determine whether LRE is an appropriate policy but rather to determine how a child can be educated in the LRE. (Girty v. School District of Valley Grove, p. 14)

As the above examples show, rationales in favor of inclusion are based upon logical, practical, and legal considerations. If it is possible to provide inclusive education with appropriate supports and services and if the courts continue to favor that it is both effective and mandated by law, why not spend our limited time, energy, and money on trying to create successful inclusion experiences rather than continue with an ineffective, segregated system?

Procedural Issues

Few would disagree that paperwork dominates special education. Nationally, special educators devote an estimated 35 to 50 percent of their time to assessments and other forms of documentation related to students' Individualized Education Program (IEP) plans (Vermont Department of Education, 1990). Unfortunately, many assessments are intended to identify, label, and categorize students rather than to gather diagnostic information for instructional purposes. Further, an extensive examination of assessment reports by Ysseldyke and colleagues (1983) revealed that they can be highly unreliable. But even if they were reliable, there is no evidence to suggest that all children assigned to a particular category (e.g., autism, Down syndrome, ADHD, gifted and talented) learn in the same way, are motivated by the same things, or have the same gifts or challenges. As teachers intuitively know, homogeneity among children who share a common label is a myth.

The huge amount of special education paperwork—timelines, meeting notices, drafts of educational goals, comprehensive reports, annual IEP reviews—serves merely as a "proxy" measure of actual student progress. For many special educators, parents, and advocates, the realization that questionable monitoring and assessment procedures are used to label a large proportion of our children has been the catalyst for demanding change in the educational system.

Population Increases

A major concern for special educators is the rising number of students identified as having disabilities. In a single 13-year period, the number of such students who were made eligible for special education rose by 23 percent

(Fuchs & Fuchs, 1994), with the number of children identified as having a learning disability increasing by 119 percent (Lipsky & Gartner, 1989). Such staggering numbers prompted the Vermont Department of Education (1993) to project that nearly *50 percent* of its students "receive services from or are eligible for a variety of special programs serving students with disabilities, economic or social disadvantages, special talents, etc." (p. 1). The question presents itself: Is it the students who have the disabilities, or the educational system?

Disjointed Incrementalism

Our system of education is not so much bifurcated as balkanized: in addition to general and special education, there are classes devoted to gifted and talented education, vocational education, bilingual education, at-risk education, and so on. All of these categories of classes are well intended, but they were also each launched separately at different times and developed incrementally. More often than not, each discrete program has its own eligibility criteria, funding formulas, and advocacy groups that sometimes conflict with those of other programs; at the very least, they result in poor coordination and duplication of services, personnel, materials, equipment, and accounting. That so many "special" programs have been created for so many children suggests that we need a unified system of education to pull all of our resources—and our children—together.

Funding

The human and financial costs of creating separate education environments can be significant. When inclusive schooling was first proposed in the early 1980s, the anticipated cost was often used as an argument against it. Since then, communities across the country have demonstrated that inclusion doesn't need to cost more at all—in fact, in many cases, the accompanying consolidation of resources, reduction of duplicate services, and elimination of bussing costs end up saving schools money that they can then invest in classroom resources for all.

Some opponents of inclusion suggest that citing the potential cost savings is inappropriate and unethical. Of course, students should not be integrated into general education classrooms for financial reasons alone—what is best for children should always be the foremost rationale. But there is nothing wrong with being fiscally responsible.

Philosophy

Some people support inclusion for deep-seated philosophical reasons: they firmly believe that the exclusion of any subgroup constitutes a violation of civil rights and of the principle of equal citizenship. These advocates see parallels in the struggles of the 1950s and 1960s, when white school officials blocked schoolhouse doors to keep black children out. They agree with Chief Justice Earl Warren's words in Brown v. Board of Education (1954) that enforced separateness in education can

> generate a feeling of inferiority as to [children's] status in the community that may affect their hearts and minds in a way unlikely ever to be undone. This sense of inferiority . . . affects the motivation of a child to learn . . . [and] has a tendency to retard . . . educational and mental development. (p. 493)

Promoters of inclusive education know that the primary factor determining whether students with disabilities will be taught separately or apart from their peers is, arbitrarily and unfairly, the community in which the students live. To create a society in which all people are valued, we must first model that society in our schools.

Demonstrations and Recognition

> *More is learned from a single success than from multiple failures. A single success proves it can be done—whatever is, is possible.*
>
> —G. J. Klopf (1979, p. 40)

Schools throughout the world are implementing inclusive practices to educate an increasingly diverse student body—including students with disabilities—in general education classrooms. Over two decades ago at the United Nations' (U.N.) 1994 World Conference on Special Needs Education, 92 nations signed the Salamanca Statement, which states in part that "education for children with special needs should be provided within the general education system, which has the best potential to combat discriminatory attitudes, create welcoming communities, and build an inclusive society" (UNESCO, 1994). Since the statement's signing, international support for inclusive education has gained momentum. At the U.N.'s 2008 International Conference on Education, 153 ministers of education and heads of delegation affirmed that "inclusive quality education is fundamental to achieving human, social, and economic development" (UNESCO, 2008).

For those who need successful demonstrations to convince them that inclusion is possible and should be considered, the mounting worldwide support for the practice can be decisive. Seeing change in action turns the question from "Can such a thing be done?" to "How can we learn from the examples and make it work in our unique community?" Observers might be influenced by the inclusion advocacy of leading national general educational organizations and of both special and regular educators. For example, in one multistate study of 680 elementary, middle, and secondary educators experienced with inclusive practices, respondents largely favored placing children with disabilities in general education environments where special and regular educators teach collaboratively, believing this practice to benefit both the students and the teachers (Villa, Thousand, Meyers, & Nevin, 1996).

Finding the Most Compelling Rationales for Change

Figure 2.3 offers a concept map of the 10 rationales for change presented in this chapter. We invite you to examine the figure and to reread sections of the chapter for clarification. Then, we invite you to answer the following two questions:

1. Personally and professionally, which of the rationales are the most compelling to you? That is, which are most likely to lead you to support a unified, inclusive educational system of general and special education?

FIGURE 2.3

Rationales for Change

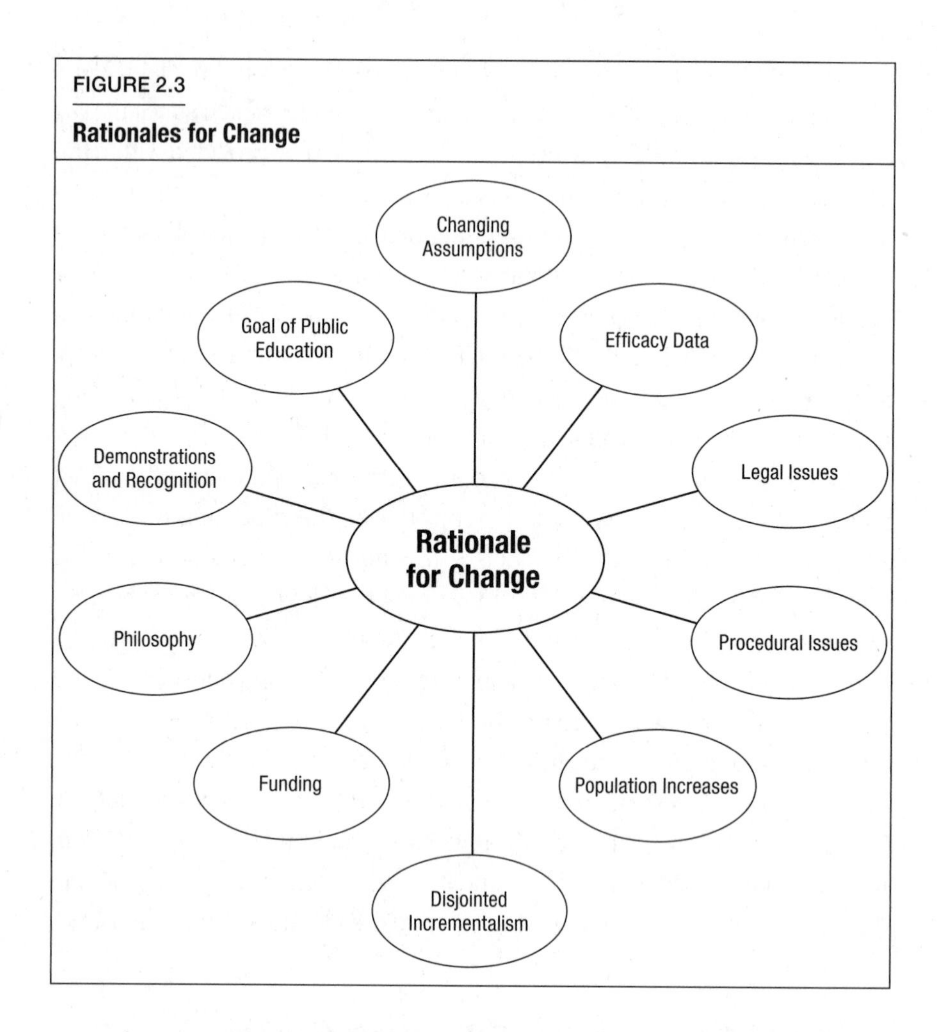

2. Which of the rationales do you think your colleagues, supervisors, students, community members, and policymakers find most compelling?

Your answers to these two questions are an important step in discerning both how beliefs and attitudes *influence* the creation of inclusive schools and how they *can be influenced* by a variety of rationales.

References

Baker, E., Wang, M., & Walberg, H. (1994). The effects of inclusion on learning. *Educational Leadership, 52*(4), 33–35.

Blackorby, J., Wagner, M., Camero, R., Davies, E., Levine, P., Newman, L., Marder, C., & Sumi, C. with Chorost, M., Garza, N., & Guzman, A. M. (2005). Engagement, academics, social adjustment, and independence. Palo Alto, CA: Stanford Research Institute. Retrieved from www.seels.net/designdocs/engagement/All_SEELS_outcomes_10-04-05.pdf.

Brendtro, L. K., Brokenleg, M., & Van Bockern, S. (2009). *Reclaiming youth at risk: Our hope for the future* (Rev. ed.). Bloomington, IN: Solution Tree.

Brown v. Board of Education of Topeka, 347 U.S. 483, 493 (1954).

Cole, D. A., & Meyer, L. H. (1991). Social integration and severe disabilities: A longitudinal analysis of child outcomes. *The Journal of Special Education, 25*(3), 340–351.

Costello, C. (1991). *A comparison of student cognitive and social achievement for handicapped and regular education students who are educated in integrated versus a substantially separate classroom* (Unpublished doctoral dissertation). University of Massachusetts, Amherst.

Freeman, S., & Alkin, M. (2000). Academic and social attainments of children with mental retardation in general education and special education settings. *Remedial and Special Education, 21*(1), 3–18.

Fuchs, D., & Fuchs, L. S. (1994). Inclusive schools movement and the radicalization of special education reform. *Exceptional Children, 60*(4), 294–309.

Ginott, H. (1972). *Teacher and child.* New York: Macmillan.

Girty v. School District of Valley Grove, 01-3934 (3rd Cir. 2002).

Glasser, W. (1986). *Control theory in the classroom.* New York: Harper & Row.

Hollowood, T., Salisbury, C., Rainforth, B., & Palombaro, M. (1995). Use of instructional time in classrooms serving students with and without severe disabilities. *Exceptional Children 61*(3), 242–253.

Individuals with Disabilities Education Improvement Act of 2004, 20 U.S.C. § 1400 *et seq.*

Kalambouga, A., Farrell, P., & Dyson, A. (2007). The impact of placing pupils with special educational needs in mainstream schools on the achievement of their peers. *Educational Research, 49*(4), 365–382.

Kelly, D. (1992). Introduction. In Neary, T., Halvorsen, A., Kronberg, R., & Kelly, D. (Eds.), *Curricular adaptations for inclusive classrooms* (pp. 1–6). San Francisco: California Research Institute for the Integration of Students with Severe Disabilities, San Francisco State.

Klopf, G. J. (1979). *The principal and staff development in the school—with a special focus on the role of the principal in mainstreaming.* New York: Bank Street College of Education.

Kunc, N. (2000). Rediscovering the right to belong. In R. A. Villa & J. S. Thousand (Eds.), *Restructuring for caring and effective education: Piecing the puzzle together* (2nd ed., pp. 77–92). Baltimore: Paul H. Brookes.

Lipsky, D., & Gartner, A. (1989). *Beyond separate education: Quality education for all.* Baltimore: Paul H. Brookes.

Maslow, A. (1970). *Motivation and personality.* New York: Harper & Row.

National Association of State Boards of Education Study Group on Special Education. (1992). *Winners all: A call for inclusive schools.* Alexandria, VA: Author.

Oberti v. Board of Education, 995 F. 2nd 1204 (3rd Cir. 1993).

Rebora, A. (2011). Keeping special ed in proportion. *Education Week*, 5(1), 36. Retrieved from www.edweek.org/tsb/articles/2011/10/13/01disproportion.h05.html.

Roncker v. Walter, 700 F.2d 1058, 1063 (6th Cir. 1983).

Sacramento City Unified School District v. Rachel H., 14 F.3d 1398 (9th Cir. 1994).

Sharpe, M. N., York, J. L., & Knight, J. (1994). Effects of inclusion on the academic performance of classmates without disabilities. *Remedial and Special Education, 15*(5), 281–287.

Strain, P. (1983). Generalization of autistic children's social behavior change: Effects of developmentally integrated and segregated settings. *Analysis and Intervention in Developmental Disabilities 3*(1), 23–34.

Straub, D. & Peck, C. (1994). What are the outcomes for nondisabled students? *Educational Leadership, 52*(4), 36–40.

Timothy W. v. Rochester, New Hampshire, School District, 825 F.2d 954 (1st Cir. 1989).

UNESCO. (1994). The Salamanca statement and framework for action on special education.

UNESCO. (2008, November) International Conference on Education, 48th session. Geneva, Switzerland. Retrieved from http://www.ibe.unesco.org/fileadmin/user_upload/Policy_Dialogue/48th_ICE/CONFINTED_48-3_English.pdf.

U. S. Department of Education. (1995). *Seventeenth annual report to Congress on the implementation of the Individuals with Disabilities Education Act.* Washington, DC: Author.

Vermont Department of Education. (1990). *Report of the special commission on special education state of Vermont.* Montpelier, VT: Vermont Department of Education.

Vermont Department of Education. (1993, February). *Vermont Act 230 three years later: A report of the impact of Act 230.* Montpelier, VT: Vermont Department of Education.

Villa, R., Thousand, J., Meyers, H., & Nevin, A. (1996). Regular and special education teacher and administrator perceptions of heterogeneous education. *Exceptional Children, 65*(1), 29–45.

Webb, N. (1994). Special education: With new court decisions backing them, advocates see inclusion as a question of values. *The Harvard Educational Letter, 10*(4), 1–3.

Ysseldyke, J., Thurlow, M., Graden, J., Wesson, C., Algozzine, B., & Deno, S. (1983). Generalizations from five years of research on assessment and decision making. *Exceptional Education Quarterly, 4*(1), 79–93.

VOICE OF INCLUSION

From My Friend, Ro Vargo

Rosalind Vargo with Joe Vargo

A school should not be a preparation for life. A school should be life.
—Elbert Hubbard

It was Tuesday, a beautiful autumn morning on the campus of Syracuse University. Ro had just finished her class "Topics in American Music—20th Century" in Bowne Hall and was walking back to the car (with my assistance) to go home. Joe, Ro's dad, was waiting in the car. He and I looked at each other and at Ro and wondered how we had gotten here. After all, it seemed like only yesterday....

Kindergarten

Among our vivid memories of Kindergarten is that of Ro's first invitation to a birthday party. Kristen's mother phoned to ask if she should make any special arrangements for Ro to attend. Fighting back tears, we responded, "No, but thanks for asking." Kristen's mom said her daughter was so looking forward to Ro coming. Then we said it: "We love Ro because she's our daughter. But do you know why other kids like her?"

"She says she likes Ro's smile," said Kristen's mom, "and that she's someone you can really talk to, and that she wears really neat clothes. I think kids like Ro because she isn't a threat to them; they can just be themselves around her."

2nd Grade

When Ro was in 2nd grade, we invited several of her classmates over to celebrate her birthday. Trying to get a head count the night before the party, we called Eric's mom and politely asked whether her son would be coming.

"I'm sorry I didn't call you," said Eric's mom. "Eric said he just told Ro in school yesterday that he was coming. Was that alright?"

It was more than alright! To Eric, the fact that Ro didn't talk didn't mean that she couldn't understand him.

A while later, while attending Mass on Sunday, we reflected on how we had worked feverishly to get Ro into regular school, but had not made the same efforts to involve her in our church community. She was regularly going to Mass now, so we thought it might be the right time to approach our pastor about having Ro receive First Communion with other children her age.

We were apprehensive when we approached the pastor, thinking we would have to justify Ro's inclusion with other students to him, so we brought a selection of scriptural references and detailed notes with us. To our surprise and delight, these were unnecessary; the pastor agreed wholeheartedly with us.

"You know," he said, "we're the ones with the hang-ups, not Ro. We make all the rules so that people like Ro can't receive Communion. I'm excited about Ro receiving our Lord, but I am even more excited about what effect Ro will have on our lives and our parish families' lives when she does."

When First Communion Day came and Ro approached the altar, Joe was paralyzed by emotion, unable to move or talk. His feelings were a testimony to what had happened not just for Ro, but for many of us there that day. The liturgy ended with hugs, kisses, tears, and a renewed belief that Christ was alive in our midst through Ro. A non-Catholic friend, unaware of the day's spiritual significance for us, said she was intensely moved by seeing Ro in a seemingly transfixed state. Her reaction brought back memories of our pastor's words about the potential impact of Ro's Communion on others' lives.

4th Grade

In 4th grade, Ro was voted "Best Friend" by her 25 "typical" classmates. Somehow, her inclusion in the school life of these kids was making a tremendous difference in their lives. Ro's gifts were recognized and celebrated.

We recall another night when we received a rare phone call for Ro. The young girl at the other end of the line said she wanted to talk to "Ro who goes to Ed Smith School."

"Hold on," I said, before turning to exclaim to Joe: "Someone wants to talk with Ro on the phone!"

We got Ro from the dinner table and put the phone to her ear. Immediately recognizing the voice of her friend Ghadeer, Ro started laughing. She then nodded her head to indicate "yes" before shaking it to indicate "no." I took the receiver and reported to Ghadeer: "Ro's listening and nodding her head."

"Great," said Ghadeer. "I'm asking her advice about a birthday present for a friend. Now, did she nod 'yes' for the jewelry or 'yes' for the board game?"

Ro's 11th Birthday

We remember with pleasure Ro's 11th birthday party. Beforehand, the mother of one of Ro's friends called me to ask if the present she had picked out for Ro was okay—she had picked it up without her daughter's input, wrapped it, and given it to her daughter to take to school that morning. She wasn't sure if the gift was the "in" thing and worried that her daughter would die of embarrassment if it weren't.

The gift was a deluxe-model jump rope. Without hesitation, I told the mom that the gift was a wonderful idea and that Ro would love using it with her sisters.

With a sigh of relief, the mom responded: "Well, I am glad. I was hoping that Ro was not disabled or anything. Is she?"

For the life of me, I wanted to say no and save this mom obvious embarrassment. In the end, I said, "Well, a little bit." After a few apologies from her and reassurances from me, we got off the phone as friends. This woman had made my day, my week, my life! The thought that an 11-year-old girl had received a birthday party invitation, wanted to go, and asked her mom to buy a present—all the while *never thinking it important to mention that her friend had a disability*—still makes me cry with wonderment and happiness.

Another message of acceptance and love came at the birthday party itself, when Ro unwrapped her friend's present. Though her friend didn't know what the present was, she did know that Ro attended occupational and physical therapy sessions three times a week.

When the jump rope was revealed, Ro's friends shrieked with elation: "Oh, cool!" "I hope I get one of those for my birthday!" The girls immediately dragged Ro down the stairs and out to the driveway, where they tied one end of the jump rope to her wrist. With the strength of her twirling partner, Ro was able to rotate the rope for her friends. It was the best adaptive occupational therapy activity she'd had in months.

A Gift for Ghadeer

Probably the most profound testimony to inclusive education occurred when Ro's friend Ghadeer suffered a cerebral hemorrhage. At the age of 12, she was comatose for almost four weeks. Teachers had prepared classmates, including Ro, for Ghadeer's imminent death. However, after weeks of having family, teachers, and friends read at her bedside, Ghadeer miraculously began to recover—though not completely: her articulation was so severely impaired that she could no longer communicate orally. To the amazement of her doctors and nurses, Ghadeer began to use sign language, which nobody knew she had learned. When an interpreter asked her how she'd come to knew it, Ghadeer signed back, "From my friend Ro Vargo!"

After four months of intensive rehabilitative therapy, Ghadeer returned to school—but now she was a "special education" student, requiring speech and language services plus physical and occupational therapy. Her family proudly reported to us that Ghadeer shunned the "special" bus and rode the "regular" bus on her first day back to school. Further, she began to advocate for herself, lobbying teachers for a laptop computer to help her with her schoolwork. Inclusive education enabled Ghadeer to get to know someone like Ro and learn both about augmentative communication systems and, more importantly, her rights—particularly her right to be a part of her school, class, and friendship circle. She had learned from Ro that people can still belong even if something unexpected, like a disability, happens to them.

What's Hard about Being Ro's Friend?

At a national education conference, Ro and a group of her friends responded to questions from parents and teachers in a session titled "Building Friendships in an Inclusive Classroom."

"I think Ro should be in class with all of us because how else is she going to learn the really important stuff?" said Tiffany. "Besides, we can learn a lot from her."

"Have you ever discussed her disability with her?" asked one of the teachers in the audience.

"No," replied Stacey. "I know Ro is different, but I never thought it was important to ask. Like, for instance, I never thought to go up to a black kid in my class and say, "'You're black. How come you're different?'"

Another teacher asked, "What is the hardest thing about being Ro's friend?" As Ro's parents, we held our breath, waiting for responses like, "She drools," "She walks funny," or "She's a messy eater."

Stacey responded: "The hardest thing about being Ro's friend is that she always has a parent or an adult with her." Ouch! That hurt. But, Stacey's observation taught us an important lesson that would have a positive effect on Ro's future.

Transition to Middle School

The transition from elementary to middle school was a tough one socially for Ro, as it can be for many adolescents. Though she attended a regular 6th grade class, she had to gain acceptance from her new peers. Initially, they tended either to ignore her or stare at her; a few even teased her. When Ro was assigned to a work group, no group members verbally complained, but Ro noticed nonverbal signs of rejection. In those first months, we began to doubt our decision to place Ro in a regular middle school class. We recalled what a teacher had said to us the year before: "Middle school kids don't like themselves. How can you expect them to like your kid?"

But soon things started to change. Ro's classmate Mauricha became the first to break through Ro's social isolation. Asked how they became friends, Mauricha said, "I saw her. She saw me. We've just been friends ever since." One night when I was taking Mauricha home, she turned to me and said, "You know, Mrs. Vargo, lots of teachers think I'm friends with Ro because it gets me more attention. That isn't true. The truth is, I need her more than she needs me."

All told, Ro's middle school experience was fairly typical. When reflecting on our other daughters' experiences in middle school, we notice many of the same issues: intermittent isolation, hot and cold friendships, a growing interest in boys, physical changes, teasing, more challenging classwork, and, of course, parents who just don't know anything.

In Ro's last year of middle school, Kristen joined her as a paraeducator. The two immediately bonded. Kristen connected with Ro in a way that no other adult had and had a real vision for her. She intuitively knew how to play the support role without getting in the way of Ro's desire to connect with others. She was more than talented—she was a gift.

That same year, Ro was assigned to Mr. S.'s gym class. Although he was initially against having Ro in his class, he eventually agreed on the condition that she stayed in the corner with Kristen. In time, several of Ro's classmates began to suspect that she was having more fun than they were and started joining her in her corner of the gym—first a few, then gradually more and more. Mr. S. soon realized that he was going to have to give in and let Ro join the regular group if his students were all gravitating toward her anyway.

On the last day of school, Ro came home with a whistle around her neck and a note from the principal that read, "Mr. S. retired today after 35 years—he wanted Ro to have his whistle."

High School

Ro and six other students with severe disabilities walked into their high school on their first day along with all of the other incoming freshmen. Early on, Ro communicated to us that she particularly enjoyed her zoology class and learned a lot from it, but that there were "some classes I didn't like. It is hard for me when classes have no small groups and no homework for me. Sometimes there is too much information. The worst is when neither the kids nor the teachers talk to me."

Despite the challenges, inclusion offered Ro a whole new world of opportunities. She joined the Key Club, accruing service hours by volunteering at an inclusive local daycare center where she also served as a role model for children with disabilities. She even got to travel to New York City for a weekend with her zoology class to visit the zoo.

During the early high school years, Ro's "voice" clarified for us what she wanted to do with her life. One night, her speech therapist phoned us to discuss the day's session. Apparently, Ro had become quite upset. She had typed something along the lines of "I want to go sitter," "Cinderella," and something about Aunt Marge, then burst out crying. These fragments made no sense to me, but they did to Joe when I told him about them.

"Don't you know what she's saying?" he said. "She's talking about when Josie went to the Christmas formal last weekend with Todd."

I didn't know if we should laugh or cry. Of course: "sitter" meant Ro's *sister,* Josie. The next morning, I asked Ro if she had been upset because she wanted to dress like Cinderella, go to a formal dance with a boy, and have Aunt Marge take pictures. She nodded her head yes. That same morning we promised Ro that she would go to her junior prom—and from the smile on her face, I think she knew that we meant it. (In the end Ro attended not only the junior prom, but also the senior ball.)

Another example of Ro's articulation providing us with insight occurred when Ro had to submit an application for her first volunteering job. A paraeducator completed the application with Ro's input. Ten minutes later, Ro dissoved into a full-blown temper tantrum.

Panicking, the paraeducator asked Ro if her tantrum had anything to do with the application. She nodded, indicating that it did. When the paraeducator went down the list of questions on the application, she noticed that she had answered one of them herself without consulting Ro: Under "What has been your biggest challenge?" the paraeducator had written "Rett syndrome." Ro wanted the line removed.

Ro also clearly expressed her thoughts when she was nominated by her teachers for Student of the Month. She had to complete an information sheet for the committee that would select the winner. After much deliberation, Ro opted not to include anything about her work with other girls who had Rett syndrome or with local university students writing papers on her life experiences. In the end, she submitted just her name, age, and the name of her favorite teacher. Ro was making it clear that she didn't think her disability was something important to share about herself. It wasn't really who she was, or what she did, or something she wanted to have.

For her Health Career class one year, Ro had to design a poster depicting the occupations she was interested in pursuing. One week we spent 15 minutes each night cutting out pictures and words for Ro and asking her if she wanted them on her poster. She would either shake her head "no" or nod back "yes" in response.

At the end of the week, the poster was finished—and it was full of the faces of people. There were no inanimate objects. Ro knew her limitations, but she also knew her strengths. She clearly wanted to work with people. Inclusive education classes were challenging Ro in every way and giving rise to a louder and louder voice.

The Voice of Ro's Peers

The voice of Ro's peers was also becoming clearer and louder with time. On the zoology class trip to New York City, Ro and her dad struggled for three days to keep up with the fast pace of a very busy itinerary. Ro's classmates seemed oblivious to her tiring easily and to the locomotion that caused her to lag behind. It appeared that they hardly noticed her at all that weekend—or at least that was Joe's observation. Still, Ro enjoyed the trip, and it was a wonderful bonding experience for her and her dad.

It was only months later that we came to understand the ramifications of Ro's participation on the trip. Without our knowledge, students who were on the trip had begun to voice concerns about Ro's support person in school. At first they complained to their teacher, telling her that they thought the assistant was disrespectful to Ro. The teacher notified the principal, but no action was taken. Frustrated, the kids told their parents, and their parents came to us. When the school administration failed to act, Ro's peers did!

Our vision of inclusive education had become a reality. We had hoped that the kids who sat in class with Ro would not seek to harm her, and they were doing more than that—they were protecting her. We now had hope that in the future they would seek the social and legislative reforms necessary to support her inclusion throughout life, and they would gladly be her friends and neighbors, happily sharing the same space as well as the same dreams.

Preparing for Higher Education

After Ro's third year in high school, she became clearly envious of her sister Josie's college planning—her campus visits and school applications. We were unclear about Ro's choices, and she communicated to us that this was not fair to her. She began to throw more temper tantrums.

Students naturally seek post-secondary opportunities. Why not Ro? At the time, the Inclusive Elementary and Special Education Program of Syracuse University (SU) and the Syracuse City School District were collaborating to enhance both SU's teacher preparation services and the school district's inclusive schooling options. The resulting ONCAMPUS program brought high school students with significant support needs aged 19 to 22 to the SU campus, where they participated with SU students in academic, social, vocational, recreational, and service-learning experiences.

After learning of ONCAMPUS, Ro's behavior improved immensely—she was happy and optimistic, and communicated with absolute delight to her classmates that she would be attending SU next year. She would even decide which courses to take, what clubs to belong to, and where she would eat lunch.

When we were securing Ro's disabled parking permit for SU, I had a conversation with a university receptionist on the phone.

"Is this permit for Ro Vargo who went to Henninger High School?" she asked me.

"Yes," I replied.

"Tell her I said hi!"

"You know Ro?"

"Yeah, I graduated with her from Henninger last year!"

Inclusive education: another voice heard and another confirmation.

College Life and Giving Back

Ro's ONCAMPUS experience resulted in an expanded network of friends. Jacqueline, a senior at SU's School of Social Work, spent time with Ro through her job as a residential habilitation counselor. She shared with Ro the names of all the good professors and generally served as a voice of experience. Jan, a sophomore in the visual and performing arts program and a member of SU's jazz, pep, and dance bands, would clue Ro in about any musical performances on campus. Before traveling abroad to study, Ashley spent every Tuesday with Ro, either grabbing a bite or just hanging out. Katie, an SU cheerleader, picked Ro up and took her to classes when her support person went on vacation. Colleen and some other friends celebrated Ro's 21st birthday with a bar-hopping adventure in a 16-passenger limo.

Justine, a senior in the Maxwell School of Communication, had seen Ro on campus and was struck by how much she reminded her of her brother, who had autism. Knowing that Ro was involved in the ONCAMPUS program, Justine approached Ro and asked if she would be willing to be a part of a short documentary for her final project highlighting her campus experience. Ro agreed, and Justine introduced her to Greg, another senior who would be codirecting the film. A year-long team relationship ensued, during which the three would meet to plan and shoot video footage. The final result, entitled *Ro,* revealed Ro's hopes and dreams as well as the realities of being on a university campus. It was respectful, serious, and funny. Many of the images showing Ro traversing the campus were searing and thought-provoking. Thanks to Justine and Greg, Ro's voice in the video will last forever.

Ro's SU experience did not end at 22, when she completed the ONCAMPUS program. Instead, a partnership between SU's Continuing Education division and Ro's adult service agency, the Access program, allowed her services to be delivered on campus and to blend in with her volunteer work (as everyone in our family, including Ro, is expected to do volunteer work). Currently, Ro volunteers for a local organization that supports housing for abused women and children and for the Red Cross (by staffing information tables at local health fairs). For years, she has visited the nursing homes of fellow parishioners. With the help of her home support staff, Ro makes holiday-themed gifts related to the time of the year that the seniors can use to decorate their rooms. She also has developed a routine of recording personalized songs and YouTube music videos on her laptop, which she plays on her visits. For an Italian parishioner, Ro records Italian songs; for her grandfather, a military veteran, she plays the Marine Corps hymn. Creating and sharing these gifts and recordings helps Ro not only communicate in new ways, but also show her generosity—a central goal of education—and the value she places in family.

Ro's nursing home visits led her to develop an interest in gerontology, so she began to take courses in the subject. Because of the many years she had spent volunteering, Ro ended up being one of the only students in her classes who had extensive experience working with senior citizens. After several years, Ro accrued enough hours in Gerontology Studies to receive a Certificate of Completion. This was a first, but not the end: in a 16-year period, Ro has completed nearly 30 SU courses. Ro continues to receive adult services at the university by taking courses at the audit rate, visiting the library, and attending campus activities.

The Future

Ro's experiences with inclusion in high school and college certainly have caused her some pain, forcing her to acknowledge her limitations and sometimes struggle to belong. Yet inclusion both in school and in the community through volunteering has also prompted Ro's self-actualization, self-determination, and self-acceptance, and has increased her confidence tremendously. Living in the "regular" world was a risk Ro was willing to take, and though it has always had both emotional and physical risks, it has clearly been worth it.

Remember Ghadeer, the girl who learned sign language from Ro? Six years after she was hospitalized, she called Ro and invited her to her high school graduation party. Mauricha, the friend who broke Ro's social barrier in middle school, sent her a note many years later that began, "Hi Ro. I know you probably don't remember me, but I have never forgotten you. I work as a home health assistant and am taking a sign language course at night." When Kristen, Ro's paraeducator, got married, Ro attended the wedding, where she and the bridal party reminisced about the last time they were all in a limo together—the night of the senior prom, some three years before. Kristen refers to Ro as the sister she never had.

Our child with "pervasive and significant support needs" has accomplished more than we ever thought possible, and she continues to grow. Also growing are those she has learned with and from through the years. We believe in these young citizens. They are Ro's community. They are the ones who will and do advocate social and legislative reform to support inclusion. They gladly are and will be good neighbors, care providers, and friends. Because of Ro's inclusion, they and Ro have experienced the four dimensions of the Circle of Courage: belonging, mastery, independence, and generosity. Now that's a life worth living!

SECTION II

Figure II.1 displays an inclusive-school framework that we call the Schoolhouse Model (Villa & Thousand, 2011). The multistory schoolhouse framework is built upon a strong foundation of administrative support. Each subsequent floor represents one or more educational best practices or school restructuring initiatives that interrelate and build upon one another to achieve overarching goals of access to and success with the general education curriculum for every child.

As the figure shows, a firm foundation of administrative leadership and support underpins the processes and initiatives on the floors above. Chapter 3 examines administrative leadership and the five variables to which district and building administrators must attend in order to facilitate change and progress in any reform initiative.

The floor immediately above the schoolhouse foundation acknowledges collaborative teaming and creative problem solving as essential processes for actualizing change. In addition to administrative support, restructuring for inclusive education depends upon school and community members collaboratively developing and using skills, processes, and time to creatively identify challenges, generate and execute solutions, and track student progress. Chapter 4 examines barriers to and elements of effective collaborative teaming and offers tools for systematically activating creativity and planning effective solutions.

The second floor of the Schoolhouse Model is shared by two organizational structures and processes for marshaling and deploying human resources to increase the likelihood of curriculum differentiation for students with diverse learning profiles. The first structure, described in Chapter 5, is a Multitiered System of Supports (MTSS) for preventing school failure and avoiding special-education referral through high-quality instruction in general education. The chapter describes how the academic support side of MTSS, known as Response to Intervention (RTI), and the behavior support side, known as Schoolwide Positive Behavior Support (SWPBS) systems, work together to promote student success through three tiers of evidence-based instruction, support, and interventions.

Also on the second floor is co-teaching, another structure for deploying human resources. Introduced in Chapter 6, co-teaching is the practice of members of a school community—general and special educators, other specialized support personnel, and students themselves—sharing instructional responsibility for all students assigned to them. Co-teaching is the form of collaboration that best supports the education of diverse learners (see Figure II.2 for other forms that are more or less intensive). Chapter 6 examines four approaches to co-teaching and offers tips for more effective practice.

Given administrative support, tools for collaborating, and structures for deploying human resources, educators are poised to engage in the third-floor practice of differentiated instruction. Differentiated instruction provides multiple pathways for students to access content, express what they know, and derive meaning from what they are learning. Chapter 7 describes and provides examples of two approaches to differentiating instruction—a reactive "retrofit" approach and the proactive Universal Design for Learning (UDL) approach.

The ultimate goal of education, represented by the top floor of the Schoolhouse Model, is access to and success in the general education curriculum for every student. Chapter 8 reminds readers of this overarching goal and offers suggestions for building a schoolhouse that welcomes, values, empowers, and supports every student's success in shared learning environments.

FIGURE II.1

The Schoolhouse Model

Top Floor	**Access and Success for All** The goal is for all students to access and succeed in the general education curriculum
3rd Floor	**Differentiated Instruction** Provides multiple pathways for students to access and interact with content and show what they know
2nd Floor	**Multitiered System of Supports (MTSS) with Response to Intervention (RTI) and Schoolwide Positive Behavior Support (SWPBS) systems** Research-based instruction and interventions to address student needs and prevent school failure
2nd Floor	**Co-Teaching** Masters of content (general educators) and masters of access (special educators and other specialists) collaboratively plan and instruct
1st Floor	**Collaborative Planning and Problem Solving** Essential processes for educators to be effective and efficient when meeting face-to-face to identify challenges and develop solutions
Foundation	**Administrative Leadership and Support** An underpinning of any change initiative is administrative leadership to articulate the *vision,* develop *skills* through professional development, provide *resources* and *incentives,* and ensure an *action plan* is crafted and activated

FIGURE II.2

Least to Most Intensive Collaborative Support Options

Consultative and Stop-in Support

Consultative support occurs when one or more adults, often including a special educator, meet regularly with classroom teachers to monitor student progress, assess the need to adapt or supplement materials or instruction, and problem solve as needed. Specialized professionals such as nurses, occupational and physical therapists, augmentative communication specialists, and guidance or career counselors often provide periodic consultation. Students also may seek assistance from consulting staff for general support or specific assignments.

Stop-in support occurs when consulting support providers stop by the classroom on a scheduled or unscheduled basis to observe student performance in the general education context, assess the need for any modifications to existing supports or curriculum, and talk face-to-face with the student, classroom teacher, and/or peers.

Co-Teaching Support

Co-teaching support occurs when two or more people share responsibility for teaching all of the students assigned to a classroom. There are four co-teaching approaches:

1. *Supportive:* One teacher takes the lead and others rotate among students to provide support.
2. *Parallel:* Co-teachers work with different groups of students in different areas of the classroom.
3. *Complementary:* Co-teachers do something to enhance the instruction provided by another co-teacher.
4. *Team:* Co-teachers jointly plan, simultaneously deliver, and equitably share responsibilities and leadership.

Individualized Support

Individualized support involves an adult, oftentimes a paraprofessional, providing support to one or more students at predetermined time periods during the day or week, or for most or all of the day. The key to successful individualized support is to ensure that the designated support person does not become "Velcroed" to an individual student, but, instead, (a) deliberately prompts natural peer supports, (b) supports the other students in the class, and (c) facilitates small group learning in heterogeneous groups. The goal is to phase out the need for individualized support by facilitating both increased student independence and increased natural support from classmates and teachers.

Finally, the second Voice of Inclusion presents the perspectives of 14 principals from exemplary inclusive schools across the nation as to how best to actualize the Schoolhouse Model.

References

Villa, R. A., & Thousand, J. S. (2011). *RTI: Co-teaching & differentiated instruction.* Port Chester, NY: National Professional Resources.

CHAPTER 3

The Foundation: Administrative Leadership and Support in Managing Complex Change

Richard A. Villa and Jacqueline S. Thousand

Why is change in organizations so difficult and so often unwelcome, even when there is overwhelming evidence that the status quo isn't working? Why do expectations for achieving both excellence and equity for *all* children in our public schools seem beyond reach or ridiculous? Why do people in the midst of a change initiative feel confusion, anxiety, or frustration? Why is administrative leadership unclear as to where to start or what direction to take with impending best practice initiatives? Why does progress occur in some places and not in others? Why has teaching not achieved the desired results for many children and youth?

Such questions have nagged us for years as we have promoted more inclusive educational options for students with and without disabilities. Though we always knew that there existed understandable ways of leading organizational change, it was only after we had gone through and observed transformations of school cultures and practices ourselves that answers began to emerge. In this chapter, we purposely do not draw absolute conclusions about or offer prescriptions for leading change for the same reasons Margaret Wheatley articulates in her assumption-shattering book, *Leadership and the New Science* (2001):

> I no longer believe that [school] organizations can be changed by imposing a model developed elsewhere. So little transfers to, or even inspires, those trying to work at change in their own organizations. . . . [T]here is no objective reality out there waiting to reveal its secrets. There

> are no recipes or formulae, no checklists or advice that describe "reality." There is only what we create through our engagement with others and with events. Nothing really transfers; everything is always new and different and unique to each of us. (pp. 8–9)

We believe, as Wheatley does, that "we have only just begun the process of discovering and inventing the new organizational forms" (p. 7) and paradigms of inclusive schools that are in sync with the diversity, rapid pace of change, and unpredictability of 21st-century life. As educational explorers and inventors, we must give up many, if not all, of our existing ideas of what does and doesn't work in schools. Einstein understood the difficulty long ago when he observed that it is impossible to solve complex problems with the same consciousness we use to create them.

The Five Variables for Managing Complex Change

To orchestrate change and progress in education, district- and building-level leaders, site-based leadership teams, department chairs, teacher union leadeship, and grade-level team leaders must attend to the following five variables:

1. Building a *vision* of inclusive schooling within a community
2. Developing educators' *skills* and confidence to be inclusive educators
3. Creating meaningful *incentives* for people to take the risk of embarking on an inclusive schooling journey
4. Reorganizing and expanding human and other *resources* for teaching diverse students
5. *Action planning* devoted to strategies for motivating staff, students, and the community to become excited about the new big picture

These variables contribute to the successful management of complex change within any organization. Studying these variables offers insight into the actions that administrators and other change leaders can take to transform schools into inclusive learning communities.

Vision

According to Schlechty, one of the greatest barriers to change in schools is the lack of a "clear and compelling set of beliefs regarding the direction of the schools and a vision of the schools that these beliefs suggest" (2009, p. 195). Building a vision, or *visionizing*, is the first variable to consider when formulating change. Unless we devote time and effort to building a common vision, many in the school and greater community may remain uncertain about the wisdom of promoting inclusion.

We like the term *visionizing* (Parnes, 1992a, 1992b) because we think an action verb suggests the active mental struggle and the "mental journey from the known to the unknown" (Hickman & Silva, 1984, p. 151) that people go through when they reconceptualize their beliefs and declare public ownership of a new view. Visionizing involves creating and communicating a compelling picture of a desired future and inducing others' commitment to that future.

Leaders of inclusive schools stress the importance of clarifying for themselves, school personnel, and the community a vision based on three basic assumptions:

- That *all* children are capable of learning,
- That *all* children have a right to an education alongside their peers, and
- That the school system is responsible for attempting to address the unique needs of *all* children in the community.

To *articulate* a vision of inclusion is necessary, but it is not sufficient. The vision must also be adopted and embraced. Visionizing requires us to foster widespread understanding and consensus about the vision, which we can do by implementing the strategies that follow.

Examining Rationales for Change

One strategy for building consensus is to educate people about the theoretical, ethical, legal, and data-based rationales for inclusive education. Recall the end of Chapter 2, where we asked the following two questions:

1. Personally and professionally, which of the rationales are the most compelling to you? That is, which are most likely to lead you to support a unified, inclusive educational system of general and special education?
2. Which of the rationales do you think your colleagues, supervisors, students, community members, and policymakers find most compelling?

Your answers to these two questions are vitally important to visionizing. Our experience tells us that to build consensus, different people find different rationales to be compelling—and each rationale is compelling to someone. Norm Kunc (personal communication, November 20, 2015) suggests that we picture each person as a circle with two halves: one half comprises concerns about a proposed change, and the other half comprises beliefs, both supportive or nonsupportive, about it. He further suggests that to shift people's beliefs in favor of change, we must first listen to and identify their concerns (i.e., questions, fears, nightmares, confusions) about the change. Next, we must use this information to determine which rationales "speak to" each individual's priority concerns. For example, fiscal and legal rationales may speak to administrators and school board members; disappointing efficacy data may speak to parents of students with disabilities and to the students themselves; and proceduralism and the disjointed or incremental nature of special service systems may speak to special educators tired of isolation and endless hours of paperwork. We can then structure opportunities to communicate support for the rationales that people find most compelling: in-service training events, book studies, distribution of readings and viewing of videos of best practices with follow-up discussions, professional learning communities (PLCs) discussions, and visits to successful inclusive schools are all good ways to do this. Finally, being knowledgeable about concerns allows us to seriously address them when planning or implementing processes by vigilantly asking, "How can we ensure that people's worst nightmares do not come true?"

Visionizing really is about replacing an old culture with a new one and managing the sense of personal loss that cultural change inevitably elicits. New heroes and heroines, new rituals and symbols must be constructed.

New traditions must replace old ones that don't work (e.g., tacking on yet another new program or professional when children with new differences arrive in school) and address educational inequities (e.g., racial and ethnic misidentification, overrepresentation and underrepresentation in separate programs such as special education or gifted and talented education) that run counter to the vision of inclusion. Of particular importance is introducing and expecting the use of new language norms, such as using "person-first" structures (e.g., "Cecilia, who happens to have Down syndrome," "Juan, who is bilingual and developing English proficiency") rather than deficit-oriented ones (e.g., "that Down syndrome girl," "that ESL kid").

Mission Statements

Another powerful strategy is to have representatives of school and community stakeholder groups examine the current district's or school's mission statement and reformulate it, if necessary, to emphasize support for all students. When people help to craft a mission statement, they feel greater ownership of it than they do when it is imposed upon them. (Although this is probably obvious, we do caution against formulating separate mission statements for special and general education programs, as this perpetuates "dual-system" thinking.)

Clearly, there are risks involved in turning over as important a function as creating a mission statement to a group of people with diverse professional and personal perspectives who are likely to differ initially in their commitment to inclusive education. However, these risks can be minimized by informing the group of the ethical, theoretical, legal, and data-based rationales for change (see Chapter 2) and by selecting at least some group members who have an in-depth understanding of inclusion and solidly support it.

Although clarifying and promoting a philosophy of inclusion in the form of a mission statement is important, we also recognize that school communities don't need to have formal statements in place to begin altering their organizational structures and instructional approaches.

Recognizing Innovators

Another way to foster consensus is by encouraging, recognizing, and publicly acknowledging staff members and students who plunge into the work of modeling and promoting inclusion early on. In doing so, it is important to ask these early adopters how they'd prefer to be acknowledged; for example, some people might find public recognition embarrassing, but would love to attend a conference on inclusion. Any person with ties to the school (e.g., bus driver, secretary, cafeteria worker, volunteer) should be a candidate for acknowledgment, because everyone has the power through word or actions to advance or impede the inclusive vision.

Identifying Visionizers

Who can or should initiate change? We suggest that anyone can be a change agent—a visionizer—regardless of where on the organizational chart they fall. What is important is that visionizers not only assist and nurture others through the change process but also steady themselves for the natural resistance that they will experience from some. They must acknowledge that change means cultural transformation, which can take many years. They must be prepared to stick around for the long haul and not quit when times get tough.

Visionizers know that their job is to create cognitive dissonance, discomfort, and a sense of urgency and even rage in the school and community. Leadership by passion works to initiate change because it helps to spark outrage in others—and as Sergiovanni (1992) puts it, "outrage tells people what is important" (p. 74). Visionizers must talk up the vision to others, persuade them to adopt it, and coach them to perform their daily schoolwork in accordance with it. Although they take every opportunity to build consensus, visionizers know that no single teaching strategy or learning style is privileged; they will vary, reflecting the unique demographics, history, and current beliefs of each community. Finally, visionizers intuitively know that change is a very personal process and that the best way to get people to take a risk on the unfamiliar is to listen to their concerns, to believe in them, and to give them the opportunities and support they need.

Skills

Unless educators believe they have the skills necessary to respond to students' and colleagues' needs, they will likely doubt their ability to be good teachers. Clearly, the more diverse the students, the more skilled educators must be as a *collective* instructional body. (Educators in a school need not all have the same content and instructional skills, but they must be able to readily access one another to share their skills across classrooms.)

Areas of Common Professional Development

No matter how exciting or promising an initiative is, educators need professional development, guided practice, feedback, and opportunities to problem solve with colleagues. For innovations such as differentiated instruction or co-teaching to become part of the new culture, people must come to understand three things:

1. How they benefit both their own personal and professional growth and the growth of their students (Hall & Hord, 2006),
2. How they contribute to attaining the overarching goal or mission, and
3. How they interface with and support other innovations to achieve the overarching goal or mission.

It is a school district's responsibility to craft a comprehensive and ongoing professional development agenda that helps people learn needed new behaviors successfully by developing their innovation-related knowledge, performance skills, and positive dispositions.

The Schoolhouse Model in Figure II.1 (see p. 45) provides a conceptual framework for creating a professional development agenda to build educator capacity for inclusive schooling. We emphasize the importance of empowering and motivating school staff in their learning by offering them a choice as to how they receive professional development (e.g., by letting them choose among live or online workshops, coaching and mentoring opportunities, co-teaching, summer institutes, book studies, and study groups).

Who Gets Professional Development?

Anyone can be a candidate for professional development and in-service training because anyone has the capacity to either support or resist inclusive education. Although initially trainings may be organized for and delivered to early adopters in the school, eventually *everyone*—teachers, administrators, paraeducators, related service personnel, secretarial and support staff, students, school board members, parents, community members—needs at least a common core of knowledge about the rationales for and benefits of inclusion. To excuse the reluctant, resistant, or apathetic will divide people, foster resentment toward nonparticipants, reinforce a "this too will pass" mentality, and generally work against the development of a unified new culture.

Professional development in support of inclusive education never ends. Not only must new staff members learn the attendant values and practices, but staff members always need to renew their practice through training so they can impart their skills to others and refine what they already do well.

Incentives

A school system can have a vision of change, personnel can have skills and abundant resources, and a plan of action can be set into motion, but without incentives that are meaningful to each person affected by the change, the outcome can be something other than excited engagement: some people might feel that their efforts are unappreciated, some may remain reluctant to take the risk of trying new things, and some may even actively resist the vision or the innovations being implemented.

Staff at schools that successfully achieve inclusion attend to the development of an *esprit de corps*—a common spirit of inspiring enthusiasm, devotion, and intense regard for the vision and honor of the group. Promoting esprit de corps requires structuring incentives according to the following guidelines:

- Attending to teams as well as individuals in order to highlight the importance of and pride in collaborative efforts

- Spending time "in the trenches" with teachers and students learning what it is they are doing well that can be publicly and privately acknowledged
- Asking staff and students what *they* each value as incentives—what is rewarding to one person may be of little significance to another
- Overlooking no one—a bus driver, secretary, or custodian can do as much to hasten the acceptance or demise of an inclusive system as an administrator or classroom teacher

Here are some ways to motivate people and reinforce words and deeds that reflect an inclusive vision:

- Sending short notes of praise (e.g., "The peer tutors from your classroom are providing very effective instruction")
- Posting thank-you letters from visitors
- Offering special training opportunities to innovators
- Asking innovators to serve as mentors for those new to inclusive education
- Asking teachers and students to tinker with and fine-tune innovations
- Providing support for travel to conferences or other schools engaged in inclusive education
- Hosting regular forums for airing concerns and generating viable solutions
- Creating and supporting opportunities to make presentations at conferences, school board meetings, parent-teacher organizations, and community gatherings
- Structuring off-campus retreats for collaborative planning efforts

Although many incentives appeal to specific individuals, the one incentive that is common and highly valued by everyone engaged in education and educational reform is *time*—especially time for shared reflection and planning with colleagues. As Raywid (1993) notes, "The time necessary to examine, reflect on, amend, and redesign programs is not *auxiliary* to teaching responsibilities—nor is it 'released time' from them. It is absolutely central to such responsibilities, and essential to making schools succeed"

(p. 34). Figure 3.1 lists ways that schools have attempted to meet the challenge of time.

FIGURE 3.1

Strategies for Expanding Time for Collaborative Planning, Teaching, and Reflection

Borrowed Time
Rearrange the school day so there is a 50- to 60-minute block of time before or after school for co-teachers to plan.
Lengthen the school day for students by 15 to 30 minutes on four days, allowing for early student dismissal on the fifth, thus gaining a long (one- to two-hour) time block for co-teachers to meet.
Common Time
Ask co-teachers to identify when during the day and week they prefer to plan and redesign the master schedule to accommodate a block for common preparation time.
Tiered Time
Layer preparation time with existing functions such as lunch and recess.
Rescheduled Time
Use staff development days for co-teachers to do more long-range planning.
Use faculty meeting time to solve common co-teaching problems of either immediate or long-range importance.
Build into the school schedule at least one co-teacher planning day per marking period or month.
Build in time for more intensive co-teacher planning sessions by lengthening the school year for teachers but not for students, or shortening the school year for students but not teachers.
Released Time
Go to year-round schooling with three-week breaks every quarter; devote four or five of the intersession days to co-teacher planning.
Freed-Up Time
Institute a community service component to the curriculum; when students are in the community (e.g., Thursday afternoon), co-teachers meet to plan.
Schedule "specials" (e.g., art, music, physical education), clubs, and tutorials during the same time blocks (e.g., first and second period) so that co-teachers have at least that extra time block to plan.

Engage parents and community members in conducting half-day or full-day exploratory, craft, hobby (e.g., gourmet cooking, puppetry, photography), theater, or other experiential programs to free up time for co-teachers to plan.
Partner with colleges and universities; have their faculty teach in the school, provide demonstrations, or conduct university-campus experiences to free up time for co-teachers to plan.
Purchased Time
Hire permanent substitutes to free up co-teachers to plan during the day rather than before or after school.
Compensate co-teachers for spending vacation or holiday time planning with pay or compensatory time during noninstructional school-year days.
Found Time
Strategically use serendipitous times that occasionally occur (e.g., snow days, student assemblies) for co-teachers to plan.
New Time
Consider ways to provide co-teachers with incentives to use their own time to plan.

Although incentives are important ingredients in any change formula, relying too heavily on *extrinsic* incentives such as honors or financial awards can interfere with the process. Sergiovanni (1990) explains:

> Traditional management theory is based on the principle "what gets rewarded gets done." . . . [Unfortunately,] when rewards can no longer be provided the work no longer will be done. Work performance becomes contingent upon a bartering arrangement rather than being self-sustaining because of moral principle or a deeper psychological connection. A better strategy upon which to base our efforts is "what is rewarding gets done." When something is rewarding it gets done even when "no one is looking." (p. 22)

Alternatives to extrinsic rewards are *intrinsic* rewards, which people respond to due to "obligations, duties, a sense of righteousness, felt commitments, and other reasons with moral overtones . . . [or because of] finding what they are doing to be personally significant in its own right" (p. 58). Intrinsic motivation among educators includes recognition of one's own increased effectiveness as evidenced by

- student development and happiness,
- pride in one's own professional risk taking and growth and the accompanying recognition from respected colleagues and students,
- personal satisfaction, or
- the experience of *flow*.

Csikszentmihayi (1990) describes flow as "the state in which people are so involved in an activity that nothing else seems to matter; the experience itself is so enjoyable that people will do it even at great cost, for the sheer sake of doing it" (p. 4). We have learned that genuine and sustainable changes in culture and dedication to inclusive schooling depend upon people who become motivated by their emotions, values, beliefs, and social bonds with colleagues rather than by outside forces.

Resources

A school system may comprise people who have a common vision, technical skills in instruction and assessment, incentives, and a sensible plan of action for change. But unless those people feel that they have the needed resources to do the job, they will likely feel discouraged, sapped of energy and enthusiasm, and drawn away from their change efforts.

Educational resources may be technical and material (e.g., paper and pencils, computer hardware and software, curriculum materials and concepts), organizational (time set aside for collaboration and planning), or human. The *human* resource—that is, the relationships among adults and children in the school and their unique gifts, talents, and trades—is arguably the most important resource for ensuring school health and improvement. Support from colleagues, students, leaders, and others in the community often is what people really are crying for when they claim to be frustrated by a lack of resources.

Redefining Roles

Teaching has been characterized as a "lonely profession" (Sarason, Levine, Godenberg, Cherlin, & Bennet, 1966, p. 74). Teachers can get the message that they're pretty much alone with their students behind the classroom door from various sources, including teacher preparation programs (e.g., solo teaching as the culminating event in clinical practice, separate programs for general and special education), the way schools are physically organized into separate classrooms for each teacher, and job descriptions and teacher evaluation procedures that emphasize individual rather than collaborative performance. Although the absurdity of teaching in isolation is obvious, the norms, traditions, and organizational structures of many schools perpetuate segregation of staff members and students as well as inflexible expectations of assigned roles (e.g., administrators, teachers, paraeducators, specialists, parents).

For educators to most readily access the resources of other staff, everyone in the school system must relinquish traditional roles, drop distinct professional labels, and redistribute their job functions across the board. Figure 3.2 shows how job functions can and have changed in schools that meld human resources by dramatically redefining roles systemwide. Flexibility and fluidity are the main aims of role redefinition; exactly who does what from one year to the next should always be subject to change and determined by the students' needs and the complementary skills and needs of educators. Because job titles and formal definitions determine how people behave, schools need to formulate new policies and job descriptions that embrace a collaborative ethic.

Co-Teaching to Merge Resources

With shifting and more fluid job functions comes the opportunity to rearrange school personnel in a variety of collaborative relationships, including mentoring and peer coaching teams, buddy systems that pair newly hired and veteran teachers, and co-teaching. Co-teaching, which we describe in depth in Chapter 6, is an arrangement of two or more members of the school or greater community who distribute the planning, instructional, and assessment responsibilities for students among themselves on a regular basis for an extended period of time. By jigsawing the unique instructional expertise, areas of curriculum background, and personal interests of formerly isolated general education and specialized educational staff, co-teaching teams bring a richer learning experience to all students, a higher teacher-to-student ratio, enhanced problem-solving capacity among educators, and more immediate and accurate diagnosis of student needs and delivery of appropriate instruction (Nevin, Thousand, & Villa, 2009; Villa, Thousand, & Nevin, 2013).

FIGURE 3.2

Changes in Job Responsibilities of School Personnel Before and After Role Redefinition

Role	Traditional Responsibilities	Redefined Responsibilities
General Education Administrator	Responsible for the management of the general education program	Responsible for the management of the educational programs for all students
	Special programs are "housed" within general education facilities, but program responsibility is that of special education rather than general education administrators	Articulates the vision and provides emotional support to staff as they experience the change process
		Participates as a member of collaborative problem-solving teams that develop solutions to barriers inhibiting the successful inclusion and education of any child
		Secures supports to enable staff to meet the needs of all children

Role	Traditional Responsibilities	Redefined Responsibilities
General Educator	Refers students who do not "fit" into the traditional program for diagnosis, remediation, and possible removal	Shares responsibility with special educators and other support personnel for teaching all assigned children and problem solving solutions when students are struggling to learn
	Teaches children who "fit" within the standard curriculum	Seeks support of special educators and other support personnel for students experiencing difficulty learning
		Collaboratively plans and teaches with other members of the staff and community to meet the needs of all learners
		Recruits and trains students to be tutors and peer buddies for one another
Special Educator	Provides instruction to students eligible for services in resource rooms, special classes, and special schools	Collaborates with general educators and other support personnel to meet the needs of all learners
		Co-teaches with regular educators in general education classes
		Recruits and trains students to be peer tutors and peer buddies for one another
Psychologist	Tests, diagnoses, assigns labels, and determines eligibility for students' admission to special programs	Collaborates with teachers to define problems and creatively designs interventions, co-teaches, provides social skills training to classes of students, conducts authentic assessments, trains students to be conflict mediators and peer tutors and buddies for one another, offers counseling to students

continued

FIGURE 3.2 *(continued)*

Changes in Job Responsibilities of School Personnel Before and After Role Redefinition

Role	**Traditional Responsibilities**	**Redefined Responsibilities**
Support Personnel and Related Service Personnel (e.g., social worker, speech and language pathologist, physical therapist)	Diagnoses, labels, and provides direct services to students in settings other than the classroom Provides support only to students eligible for a particular special program	Assesses and provides direct services to students within general education classrooms and community settings Supports students not eligible for special education Trains classroom teachers, instructional assistants, volunteers, and students to carry out support services Shares responsibility for meeting the needs of all students
Paraeducator/Paraprofessional (instructional assistant)	Works in separate programs If working in general education classrooms, stays in close proximity to and works only with students eligible for special services	Provides services to a variety of students in general education settings Facilitates natural peer supports within general education settings
Student	Primarily works independently and competes with other students for "best" performance Passively receives learning	Often works with other students in cooperative learning arrangements Is actively involved in instruction, advocacy, and decision making for themselves and one another

The Administrator's Role as a Resource

School administrators are a critical resource to educators, as Littrel, Billigsley, and Cross (1994) discovered when they examined the effects of principal support on general and special educators' stress, job satisfaction, school commitment, health, and intent to stay in the profession. They found that administrators offer four different types of support:

- *Instrumental*—helping teachers with their work,
- *Appraisal*—offering coaching and feedback or clarifying job responsibilities,
- *Informational*—providing professional development and current updates on best practices, and
- *Emotional*—showing teachers that they are esteemed and worthy of concern through "open communication, showing appreciation, taking an interest in teachers' work, and considering teachers' ideas" (p. 297).

Of the four types, emotional support from administrators emerged in Littrel, Billingsley, and Cross's study as the one with the greatest effect on educators.

Administrators also serve as resources when they reorganize teachers' lives through a flexible and responsive master schedule that enables them to meet and teach as teams. To properly coordinate the elements of the schedule, they must first ask teachers to identify the various peer collaborations that they are currently involved in, or that they would like to structure, and then ensure that they don't conflict with schoolwide functions such as faculty meetings, curriculum development meetings, grade-level team meetings, MTSS meetings, or in-service training events. Administrators can also work with teachers and the community to modify the master schedule to create more time (in ways such as those identified in Figure 3.1) for face-to-face interactions and meaningful collaborations that advance inclusive education.

Students as Resources

The terms *co-teaching* and *collaboration* usually conjure up images of adults joining forces with one another. However, many inclusive schools have also discovered the importance of teachers sharing their instructional and decision-making power with students in a climate of mutual respect. Among the limitless collaborative structures that benefit students and educators alike are those that involve students

- as instructors in partner learning, cooperative group learning, and adult-student co-teaching arrangements (Villa, Thousand, & Nevin, 2010);
- sitting on their own and their classmates' IEP and transition-planning teams to advocate for their own or their classmates' interests; and
- sharing decision-making responsibilities by serving on curriculum and discipline committees or on the school board.

Outside Partnerships

Developing partnerships with state education department personnel, faculty at institutions of higher education, and other school districts with an interest in inclusive education can gain schools much-needed human, political, and fiscal resources:

- State education department personnel may provide fiscal incentives or regulatory relief for innovations related to inclusion as well as valuable public relations support through publications and public presentations.
- Collaborations between schools or districts and institutions of higher education can be mutually beneficial. Together, both parties can design and solicit state or federal support for model demonstrations; arrange for valuable clinical practice and internship experiences for students in teacher preparation programs; conduct research to document the challenges, solutions, and effect of inclusive schooling practices; and codevelop and deliver workshops or coursework to foster new roles and skills (e.g., co-teaching) necessary for inclusion to succeed.
- Schools sharing a common vision of inclusive education can exchange resources including personnel (e.g., by jointly hiring them), work together to address barriers to change, form coalitions to advocate for updating state funding formulas and policies, and celebrate their successes with one another.

Action Planning

For any school initiative to be successfully realized, administrators must have an action plan in place to activate the other four variables discussed in this chapter—vision, skills, incentives, and resources. Action planning means attending to the four variables and being thoughtful and transparent about the *process* of change—that is, how, with whom, and in what sequence the steps of change are formulated, communicated, and set into motion. Action planning can be tricky as it requires the right mix of planning and action and the continual involvement of the many people affected by the change.

The Right Mix without Overplanning

Alex Osborn (1993), a pioneer in the field of creativity, is known for noting that a fair idea put into action is much better than a good idea left on the polishing wheel. He recognized that it is possible to literally plan something to death—that unless planning quickly leads to action, interest will wane. Schlechty (2009) acknowledges the same concern when suggesting that we take a "ready, fire, aim" rather than a "ready, aim, fire" approach to planning change initiatives. People must be comfortable with the unknown and be able to go with the flow. Throughout the change process, they must accept that expectations about how long it will take, what the exact steps will be, and precisely how things will finally look must be continuously readjusted.

Principles of Systematic Planning

Though school districts should resist the urge to overplan, it is still very important that they have a planning *process* in place. Action plans for change can take many forms and may employ any of a number of decision-making processes (e.g., strategic planning). Whatever process a district adopts must lead to regular, observable, and measurable action. Here are some guiding principles for planning to bear in mind:

- *Do not plan in a vacuum; look outside.* Knowing about social, political, cultural, and economic trends outside the world of school is critical to seeing the change initiative as contemporary and relevant.

- *Look inside, too.* Carefully examine existing strengths and weaknesses related to school policies, practices, organizational structures, and personnel.
- *Include all stakeholders.* Ensure that all relevant stakeholder categories (e.g., teachers, parents, the teachers' union, community members, students) are represented in the planning process and that they receive regular updates.
- *Monitor the change.* Change is dynamic—the forces that drive and restrain it shift over time, and its consequences are unpredictable. For this reason, planning teams should meet regularly to review progress, revise and modify plans, disband groups that have accomplished their tasks, and create new groups to develop additional strategies.
- *Revisit the vision.* The district's vision of inclusion can get lost or distorted over time, and new arrivals may be unaware of it or misunderstand it. Leaders should keep everyone on track by periodically reexamining the vision and using media (e.g., school newsletters, the school district's website, newspaper articles, TV spots) to reinforce it.
- *Put things in writing.* People implement change best when their choices are spelled out in a systematic written format that specifies in detail who will do what, by when, and according to what criteria (i.e., an action plan).

Involvement and Communication

Engaging all stakeholders in action planning helps them to develop a sense of ownership over the coming changes and faith that change really *will* occur. Planning is the alarm signaling to everyone that things no longer will be the same; visionizers must effectively communicate desired outcomes and clearly show how everyone will play a role in making them come to life. Sometimes visionizers with the strongest sense of purpose and most brilliant intuitions about what needs to be done have trouble showing others how change will take place. They end up imposing strategies and appearing authoritarian—not because they wish to, but because they are the only ones who see the decisions that need to be made. Visionizers must not only conceptualize their strategic insights but also make them public knowledge so they can be understood, challenged, and further improved.

Healthy Assumptions

In healthy organizations, people examine their subconscious assumptions about how things operate—and the same is true of a healthy change effort. In addition to attending to the five complex change variables, we encourage facilitators engaged in action planning to adopt the following five healthy assumptions, which Fullan and Stiegelbauer (1991) assert are essential for the success of any action plan:

1. No single individual's conception of change is necessarily the one that will or should result.
2. No amount of knowledge ever clarifies what actions are "correct."
3. Manageability is achieved by thinking big and starting small.
4. Lack of participation or commitment does not necessarily reflect a rejection of the vision for change; other factors, such as insufficient skills, incentives, or resources, may be to blame.
5. Changing the culture, not implementing an innovation, is the real agenda.

Evaluation

Regular and continuous evaluation is integral to action planning. Clearly, we want to know whether inclusion is working. Are students with and without disabilities achieving academic and social success? Are they experiencing the elements of the Circle of Courage—belonging, mastery, independence, and generosity? What outcomes are students experiencing when they leave school (e.g., employment, continuing education, civic contributions)? Evaluations should also reveal affective and process variables, such as educators' feelings at various points during the change process and what Hall and Hord (2006) refer to as "stages of concern" (e.g., from little involvement, to informational and personal concerns, to implementation and refinement concerns).

Evaluations offer change agents the information they need to adjust their action plans so that they address concerns, failures, confusions, and successes as they develop. Any question that is important for a stakeholder to pose is worthy of answering through evaluation. The evaluation agenda should also be as flexible and open as the planning process, as unexpected outcomes are not uncommon. *Case in point:* a friend of ours who attended segregated special education classes in elementary school experienced a *25-point increase* in her tested cognitive abilities following two years of inclusive education classes in secondary school.

Final Thoughts

The difficult we do immediately; the impossible takes a little longer.
—Army Corps of Engineers motto during World War II

We now know enough about change that transitioning to inclusive schooling no longer seems impossible. We know that schools have cultures, and that actualizing a new vision means replacing an old culture with a new one. We know that change inevitably creates cognitive and interpersonal conflict that can be managed through perspective taking and creative problem solving. We know that fundamental change occurs when the roles, rules, relationships, and responsibilities of everyone—students included—are redefined. Hierarchical power relationships must be altered so that all stakeholders have a voice and role in decision making. We know that change is not necessarily progress; only close attention to valued outcomes will tell us if it is. We know that action planning is important and that resources, incentives, and skill building make a difference. We know that people often don't commit to change until they develop skills and experience with it, and that initial negative or neutral feelings toward inclusion can and do change.

Clearly, the complex nature of reengineering schooling can be difficult. Yet an increasing number of communities have taken the plunge and implemented a vision of inclusive education with integrity and quality. Effective inclusive school systems can be crafted by individuals who are able to use what they know about change processes to steward a larger vision.

References

Brendtro, L. K., Brokenleg, M., & Van Bockern, S. (2009). *Reclaiming youth at risk: Our hope for the future* (Rev. ed.). Bloomington, IN: Solution Tree.

Csikszentmaihalyi, M. (1990). *Flow: The psychology of optimal experience.* New York: HarperCollins.

Fullan, M. G., & Stiegelbauer, S. (1991). *The new meaning of educational change* (2nd ed.). San Francisco: Jossey-Bass.

Hall, G., & Hord, S. (2006). *Implementing change: Patterns, principles and potholes* (2nd ed.). Boston: Allyn & Bacon.

Hickman, C., & Silva, M. (1984). *Creating excellence: Managing corporate culture, strategy, and change in the new age.* New York: New American Library.

Littrell, P. C., Billingsley, B. S., & Cross, L. H. (1994). The effects of principal support on special and general educators' stress, job satisfaction, school commitment, health, and intent to stay in teaching. *Remedial and Special Education, 15*(5), 297–310.

Nevin, A. I., Thousand, J. S., & Villa, R. A. (2009). *A guide to co-teaching with paraeducators: Practical tips for K–12 educators.* Thousand Oaks, CA: Corwin.

Osborn, A. (1993). *Applied imagination: Principles and procedures of creative problem solving* (3rd rev. ed.). Buffalo, NY: Creative Education Foundation.

Parnes, S. J. (1992a). *Source book for creative problem solving: A fifty-year digest of proven innovation processes.* Buffalo, NY: Creative Education Foundation.

Parnes, S. J. (1992b). *Visionizing: State-of-the-art processes for encouraging innovative excellence.* Buffalo, NY: Creative Education Foundation.

Raywid, M. A. (1993). Finding time for collaboration. *Educational Leadership, 51*(1), 30–34.

Sarason, S., Levine, M., Godenberg, I., Cherlin, D., & Bennet, E. (1966). *Psychology in community settings: Clinical, educational, vocational, and social aspects.* New York: John Wiley & Sons.

Schlechty, P. (2009). *Leading for learning: How to transform schools into learning organizations.* San Francisco: Jossey-Bass.

Sergiovanni, T. J. (1990). *Value-added leadership: How to get extraordinary performance in schools.* Orlando, FL: Harcourt Brace Jovanovich.

Sergiovanni, T. J. (1992). *Moral leadership: Getting to the heart of school improvement.* San Francisco: Jossey-Bass.

Villa, R. A., Thousand, J. S., & Nevin, A. I. (2010). *Collaborating with students in instruction and decision making: The untapped resource.* Thousand Oaks, CA: Corwin.

Villa, R. A., Thousand, J. S., & Nevin, A. I. (2013). *A guide to co-teaching: New lessons and strategies to facilitate student learning* (3rd ed.). Thousand Oaks, CA: Corwin.

Wheatley, M. J. (2001). *Leadership and the new science: Discovering order in a chaotic world* (2nd ed.). San Francisco: Berrett-Koehler Publishers.

CHAPTER 4

Collaborative Planning and Problem Solving

Jacqueline S. Thousand and Richard A. Villa

A variety of problem-solving teams that promote inclusion exist within schools. The co-teaching teams described in Chapter 6 engage in instructional planning and problem solving for their students as part of their recursive planning-teaching-reflecting cycle. IEP planning teams exist for students eligible for special education. Most every school has a general education problem-solving team that might go under any of various names—child study team, student study team, student success team, MTSS/RTI team—but their function is always to support classroom teachers, address issues with individual students, and prevent unnecessary referrals for special education eligibility assessment. Other types of common school teams include positive behavior support teams, professional development teams, and professional learning communities.

Common to all of these partnerships is the need to develop and practice effective and efficient collaborative planning and problem solving. In a national study of over 600 general and special education teachers and administrators, Villa, Thousand, Nevin, and Meyers (1996) found collaboration to be one of the top three predictors, along with administrative support and professional development, of positive attitudes toward inclusive education. Likewise, the National Center on Educational Restructuring and Inclusion (1996) found that the availability of opportunities to collaborate (e.g., by attending team meetings, planning together and co-teaching, or meeting with parents) is critical to successful inclusion.

Emerging data suggest that educators who collaborate on planning and teaching with one another and with students' families can expect improvements in the academic and social skills of students with disabilities and other learning and language differences. The Individuals With Disabilities Education Improvement Act (IDEIA) of 2004 makes this clear:

> Almost 30 years of research and experience [have] demonstrated that the education of children with disabilities can be made more effective by . . . having high expectations for such children and ensuring their access to the general education curriculum in the regular classroom . . . and ensuring that families of such children have meaningful opportunities to participate in the education of their children . . . [and by] providing appropriate special education and related services and aids and supports in the regular classroom to such children, whenever possible. (P.L. 108–446, Part B, Sec. 682 [c] Findings [5])

Educators who jointly plan and make decisions capitalize upon the unique and specialized knowledge and skills of their teammates (Hourcade & Bauwens, 2002), experience increased higher-level thinking, and generate more novel solutions (Thousand, Villa, Nevin, & Paolucci-Whitcomb, 1995)—they are activating the "two heads are better than one" phenomenon of *synergy*. These educators also feel empowered because collaboration allows them to meet their basic human needs of survival, power, freedom of choice, sense of belonging, and fun (Glasser, 1999): The chances of *survival* and increased *power* increase through the exchange of resources and expertise, feelings of *belonging* and *freedom* from isolation blossom during collaborative planning, and the process of engaging in stimulating conversation and creative solution finding with fellow adults is *fun*.

Barriers to Effective Teaming and Problem Solving

The overarching responsibilities of any school planning team are to solve identified problems and to plan and implement supports and services for students, yet research findings suggest that they often fall short in this regard. Newton and colleagues (2014) examined the literature on the barriers and facilitators of effective teaming to support students with high-incident disabilities; Ryndak, Lehr, Ward, and DeBivoise (2014) did the same for teams supporting students with low-incident disabilities. Together, the two reviews identified barriers related to lack of face-to-face interaction (incomplete team membership, attendance challenges); to team cohesion, positive interdependence, and social interaction (disagreements about team goals, lack of parity among group members, lack of clearly defined roles); and, most commonly, to accountability (absence of a well-defined problem-solving process, lack of follow-through, ignorance of potentially revealing data).

In *Conceptual Blockbusting: A Guide to Better Ideas* (2001), James Adams identifies perceptual, cultural, and emotional barriers or blocks that people commonly experience when attempting to solve problems. Perceptual blocks identify rules that don't exist or prevent us from being able to imagine situations from different perspectives. One well-known example of a perceptual block is the one that afflicted the president of the Michigan Savings Bank when he advised against investing in the Ford Motor Company on the grounds that "the horse is here to stay; but the automobile is only a novelty —a fad" (cited in Goleman, Kaufman, & Ray, 1993, p. 128). Cultural blocks include unspoken beliefs that playfulness, humor, fun, and wild ideas are incompatible with the critical thinking and seriousness necessary for problem solving. Emotional blocks, though possibly the most common, are also the hardest to notice. These include the fear of failure or of sounding foolish or different, biases toward quick conclusions over mulling matters over, and tendencies to judge rather than generate ideas—all of which can serve to stifle a team's creativity.

If teaming is so good for teachers and students, how do we overcome these barriers and get more of it going? In this chapter, we offer theoretical frameworks, tools, and strategies for overcoming barriers and enhancing team effectiveness, efficiency, and creativity in planning and executing solutions to problems.

Elements of Effective Teaming

Our understandings of effective teaming are largely drawn from firsthand experiences with inclusive schools and the teams that support them (Villa & Thousand, 2005) and our reading of the literature on cooperative group learning (Johnson & Johnson, 2009), collaboration and consultation (Hourcade & Bauwens, 2002), and cooperation (Brandt, 1987). An effective collaborative team may be defined as two or more people who agree to do the following four things:

1. Coordinate their work to achieve at least one *common, publicly agreed-on* goal (e.g., improved student outcomes). Members of the most successful teams spend time upfront discussing and agreeing on shared goals. In doing so, they learn the power of combining their unique expertise, skills, and resources.
2. Demonstrate *parity* by alternating between the roles of teacher and learner, expert and novice, giver and recipient of knowledge. Parity occurs when members perceive that their unique contributions to the team are valued. Team members must overcome any cultural or emotional blocks preventing them from exchanging their concerns freely, regardless of differences in knowledge, skills, attitudes, or rank. Soliciting opinions and being sensitive to teammates' suggestions is especially important for members whose statuses may be perceived as unequal. For example, a teacher might use her instructional expertise to help a principal solve a curriculum redesign challenge, and a principal might be able to recommend school or external behavior supports for a teacher's student.
3. Use a *distributed functions theory of leadership* whereby the functions of the traditional solitary teacher are distributed among all co-teaching team members. Team members who deliberately redistribute leadership roles among themselves have a greater sense of interdependence. Multiple functions can be translated into concrete team roles that are rotated over time (see Figure 4.1).

FIGURE 4.1

Facilitating Task Achievement and Relationship Development

Task Roles

Timekeeper: Monitors the time, encourages planning team members to stop at agreed-upon times, and alerts members when the end of the agreed-upon time period is approaching (e.g., "We have five minutes left to finish.")

Recorder: Writes down the decisions made by the team and distributes copies to present and absent team members.

Summarizer: Summarizes outcomes of a discussion before moving on to a new topic.

Checker: Makes sure members understand discussion and decisions (e.g., "Can you explain how we arrived at this decision?")

Relationship Roles

Encourager: Encourages all team members to participate and carry out their roles.

Praiser: Lets members know when they are using collaborative skills that positively affect each other with authentic and focused rather than general comments (e.g., "Thanks to [name] for keeping us focused on our tasks!" rather than "Good job!")

Jargon Buster: Lets team members know when they are using terms that not all participants may understand, such as acronyms or abbreviations (e.g., "Whoops! Does everyone know what IEP means?")

4. Use a *cooperative process.* There are five key elements to successful cooperative processes: positive interdependence; group interpersonal skills; group processing; individual accountability; and frequent face-to-face interactions. More on each of these elements follows.

Positive Interdependence

Positive interdependence is at the heart of effective teaming and involves recognizing that no single person can meet the diverse psychological and educational needs of all students. Team members create the feeling of positive interdependence when they agree to share problem-solving responsibilities by pooling together their knowledge, skills, and material resources. To establish positive interdependence, team members can and should agree on common goals, celebrate efforts and successes, and share the work of planning, implementing, and assessing proposed solutions. Rotating leadership functions among team members also helps to create a sense of positive interdependence.

Group Interpersonal Skills

Effective teams have members who pay conscious attention to practicing and improving their interpersonal skills and relationships. Verbal and nonverbal interpersonal skills include trust, trust building, conflict management, and creative problem solving, and all are necessary for leadership functions to be equitably distributed. Team members often find that they function at different interpersonal skill levels depending on their training, mastery of curriculum content, personality styles, communication preferences, and how many teammates they have.

Most people develop proficiency in teaming by actually working with and getting to know their teammates. An initial step, then, is to devote some meeting time to learning about teammates' cultural, personal, and professional backgrounds, as well as each member's experiences with teaming. Tapping into one another's unique cultural heritages also helps members learn about their teammates' strengths and interests.

It also helps team members to know that working with others to plan and evaluate lessons is a multistage developmental process. Knowing what is expected of them can help teammates learn and choose to use specific interpersonal and communication skills that help both to accomplish goals and to maintain positive relationships.

Trust building and establishing norms. When teams first form, the initial goal is to build reciprocal relationships among team members. The interpersonal skills that facilitate this goal include trust-building behaviors such as arriving on time and staying for the entire meeting. At this stage, teams must agree upon common goals and establish norms or ground rules (e.g., no put-downs, use each person's preferred name). Norms are "a group's common beliefs regarding appropriate behavior for members; they tell, in other words, how members are expected to behave. . . . All groups have norms, set either formally or informally" (Johnson & Johnson, 2005, p. 424). By explicitly stating and committing to norms, team members create a sense of safety that allows each of them to share information with one another and speak honestly about needs and concerns.

Communication and leadership. Once groups have established a sense of trust, team members can focus upon communication and leadership skills that enable them to efficiently meet goals while further developing their relationships with one another. These skills include clarifying or explaining one's own views, coordinating tasks, accurately paraphrasing the views of others, and checking for understanding and agreement with team decisions, and they are most effective when well defined and when members' roles rotate from one meeting to the next. To help planning teams begin practicing communication and leadership skills, we encourage consulting the leadership roles listed in Figure 4.1—and creating additional roles as you need them.

Creative problem solving. Creative problem-solving skills include generating novel ideas (i.e., brainstorming), seeking additional information through questioning, metacognition, asking about the underlying rationale for an argument or proposal, requesting critical feedback, trying unfamiliar practices in order to deepen understanding of new information, and taking risks simply to try something new without knowing whether it will work. Later in this chapter we discuss Sid Parnes' (1992a, 1992b) Creative Problem-Solving Process, which has been found to be particularly useful in providing teams with structured planning for highly creative people and in busting perceptual blocks to creative thinking (see p. 81).

Conflict resolution. Conflict is inevitable within all teams, especially when the goals are as important as ensuring the academic, social, and emotional success of all students. Collaborative team members who can engage in and comfortably manage conflicting opinions are more successful than those who avoid them. The skills involved in engaging constructively with conflict include criticizing ideas, not people; differentiating different opinions; asking for more information and an underlying rationale to understand someone else's position; and using creative problem-solving techniques. Practicing these skills allows for the clashing of ideas to stimulate revision and refinement of existing instructional methods, enhances a team's cohesiveness, and allows a team to reach its highest potential.

Group Processing

Group processing refers to regular time built into each meeting for members to check in with one another and determine whether problem-solving ideas are working and whether teammates are maintaining and developing interpersonal relationships. Methods of self-monitoring and processing vary from simple to complex. Some teams use checklists to keep track of agreed-upon roles and responsibilities; others have members take turns sharing accomplishments, reporting on their individual contributions, and suggesting improvements.

Individual Accountability

Individual accountability is the engine of collaboration: it serves as a way of acknowledging the importance both of everyone's individual actions and of the team as a whole. It requires members to assess the discrete performance of each team member for one or more of the following reasons:

- To help members better understand their contributions to the work of the team,
- To recognize members' contributions,
- To determine whether any roles or actions need adjusting, or
- To determine whether any members need help (e.g., coaching, access to additional resources or supports) to better perform their responsibilities.

Face-to-Face Interactions

Frequent and predictable face-to-face interaction is vital to maintaining decision-making continuity, monitoring how team decisions are implemented, and adjusting action plans in a timely fashion. Teams are most efficient when they agree beforehand on when and how often to meet and how long meetings will be. They also need to decide when others (e.g., parents, specialists, paraprofessionals, psychologists) should be involved and to develop a system for communicating information when formal meetings are not scheduled.

Team membership. We have found that optimally effective teams include members who

- have the needed expertise to solve the problem at hand (e.g., assistive technology specialists, behavior support specialists, English language learning teachers, math coaches),
- have direct experience with the students on whose behalf the meeting was convened (e.g., parents, classroom teachers, paraeducators),
- are affected by the decisions that the team is making (e.g., those on behalf of whom the meeting was convened, paraeducators who will help implement the solutions), and
- have an interest in and are invited by those on behalf of whom the meeting was convened (e.g., friends, siblings, classmates, grandparents).

Making time for face-to-face interaction. Time is a finite resource that must be planned out and allocated as efficaciously as possible—after all, it is the basic dimension through which the work of teams is constructed and evaluated. Time often defines the possibilities and limitations of a team. (Refer to Figure 3.1 in Chapter 3 for some common ways school teams have of meeting time challenges.)

Using a structured agenda to increase efficiency. Meetings are more likely to be both effective and efficient when members consistently use a structured agenda to guide their conversations. The format in Figure 4.2 ensures that teams attend to the five key elements of the cooperative process—positive interdependence, group interpersonal skills, group processing, individual accountability, and frequent face-to-face interactions—when they meet (Thousand & Villa, 2000):

- *Positive interdependence.* Roles are rotated and assigned in advance of the next meeting so that members can collect the materials they will need.
- *Group interpersonal skills.* Pauses are built in for *group processing* at the halfway point and at the end of the meeting.
- *Individual accountability.* Members are assigned tasks with corresponding due dates.

FIGURE 4.2

Collaborative Planning Meeting Agenda Form

People present:	Absentees:	Others who need to know:
Roles	**This Meeting**	**Next Meeting**
Timekeeper		
Recorder		
Other:________________		

Agenda	
Agenda Items	Time Limit
1. Review agenda and positive comments	5 minutes
2.	
3.	
4. Pause for group processing of progress toward task accomplishment and use of interpersonal skills	2 minutes
5.	
6.	
7. Final group processing of task and relationship	

Minutes of Outcomes		
Action Items	*Person(s) Responsible*	*By When?*
1. Communicate outcomes to absent members and others by:		
2.		
3.		

Agenda Building for Next Meeting		
Date: ________	Time: ________	Location: ________
Expected Agenda Items		
1.		
2.		
3.		

- *Face-to-face interactions.* Members are recorded as being present, late, or absent from the meeting.

Team Collaboration Checklist

Team members can use the checklist in Figure 4.3 to periodically check their team's "health" and plan for improvements. We suggest that each team member first individually rate the checklist items before the group completes the checklist as a whole. The team should only check "Yes" on an item if all members unanimously voted that way individually. This approach encourages team members to have a real dialogue about their different perceptions. We hope teams have fun using this checklist to celebrate their growth and to remind all members of the components that make an effective team truly productive and enjoyable.

The Stages of the Osborn-Parnes Creative Problem-Solving Process

The Osborn-Parnes Creative Problem-Solving Process, or the CPS process, enables users to generate commitments for implementing solutions with integrity and to develop lifelong creative dispositions (Parnes, 1992a). The process has been extensively applied in business and education over the past several decades. The six stages of it that we discuss in this chapter are based on a synthesis of the work of Alex Osborn (1993/1953) and his

FIGURE 4.3

Team Collaboration Checklist

Directions: Check Yes or No for each of the following statements to determine your collaboration score at this point in time.

Yes	*No*	*In our team planning and problem-solving team:*
Positive Interdependence		
		1. Have we publicly discussed the group's overall purpose and goals?
		2. Do we distribute leadership responsibility by rotating roles (e.g., recorder, time-keeper, encourager, agreement-checker)?
		3. Do we start each meeting with positive comments and devote time at each meeting to celebrate successes?
		4. Do we have fun at our meetings?
Group Interpersonal Skills and Individual Accountability		
		5. Have we established norms for behavior during meetings (e.g., all members participate, active listening when others speak, no "scapegoating")?
		6. Do we explain the norms to new members?
		7. Do we create a safe atmosphere for expressing genuine and potentially contradictory perspectives and do we acknowledge conflict during meetings?
		8. Do we have a communication system for absent members and people who need to know about our decisions, but who are not regular team members (e.g., building or district administrators)?
		9. Do we consciously identify our decision-making process (e.g., consensus, unanimous decision, CPS) for making a particular decision?
Group Processing		
		10. Do we consciously attempt to improve our interpersonal skills (e.g., perspective-taking, creative problem solving, conflict resolution) by setting time aside to reflect upon and discuss our interactions and feelings?
		11. Do we consciously attempt to improve our interpersonal skills by setting interpersonal goals for our next meeting time?

Face-to-Face Interaction		
		12. Do we hold regularly scheduled meetings at times and locations agreed upon in advance by teammates?
		13. When we meet, do we arrange ourselves so we can see and hear each other?
		14. Do we use a structured agenda format that prescribes and identifies agenda items for the next meeting and sets time limits for each agenda item?
		15. Are needed members invited? Do they receive a timely invitation? (Note: Needed members change from meeting to meeting based upon agenda items.)
		16. Do we start and end on time?
		TOTAL

protégé, Sid Parnes (1992a, 1992b); Giangreco and colleagues (1992); and ourselves (Villa, Thousand, & Nevin, 2009).

Each stage of the CPS process begins with *divergent* thinking activities—the broad exploration of possible ideas and actions—and ends with *convergent* thinking activities—the sorting, organizing, evaluating, and selecting of preferred ideas or actions. Parnes (1992a) identifies the ability to easily move back and forth between divergent and convergent thinking as an attribute of highly creative people (Parnes, 1992a, 1992b).

Stage 1: Challenge Finding

Teams are on the lookout for situations in need of improvement. They first engage in divergent thinking and consider a variety of possible challenges. Then they switch to convergent thinking and select a single challenge on which to focus that can be solved in the time allocated.

Stage 2: Fact Finding

Teams start with divergent thinking, asking questions, and collecting data about the challenge. They record and save all facts. If two people have contradictory perceptions about the exact same event, both perceptions should be recorded. The stage ends when problem-solvers sort, organize, and review the data most relevant to the challenge.

Stage 3: Problem Finding

Teams clarify the challenge by considering it from different perspectives. Members identify issues related to the challenge and turn them into positive, solvable statements by using "In what ways might we . . . " as a starter phrase. For example, if the challenge is that teachers don't have enough time to plan together, issues might be restated as follows: In what ways might we . . .

- use part of a professional development day for time to plan?
- hire a permanent substitute teacher to cover for us twice a month?
- rearrange our schedule so we have a common preparation period?
- schedule "specials" (e.g., art, music, physical education), clubs, and tutorials during the same time blocks (e.g., first and second period) so that teachers have that extra time block to plan?
- engage parents and community members in conducting half-day or full-day experiential programs such as theater or photography to free up planning time?

Each of the above statements points to different potential solutions to the challenge. By breaking challenges into component parts, it is possible to generate bite-sized actions to address each part. Team members consider the consequences of the identified actions and, thinking convergently, select the most promising one to tackle as a group.

Stage 4: Idea Finding

Team members brainstorm to generate possible solutions to the problem. Osborn first described the process of brainstorming in his book *Applied Imagination: Principles and Procedures of Creative Thinking* (1953/1993). Brainstorming requires adherence to the following five rules:

1. *Quantity is foremost—the more ideas, the better.* Avoid talking about details, as it slows down the process. Details come later.
2. *Freewheeling is welcomed.* Wild ideas are encouraged. Critical examination comes later.

3. *No negative reactions to ideas are allowed.* Premature judgments interrupt the flow of ideas and can prevent the expression of new ones.
4. *Keep it short.* A few minutes is about as long as the mind can stay intensely creative in a group.
5. *Assign a recorder.* This team member's job is to quickly jot down key words or phrases to represent each idea. Because recording should never slow down the generation of ideas, it may help to have two people writing things down.

Brainstorming helps to clear out the cobwebs, so to speak, and make way for novel ideas. One good strategy is to try to make each new idea as different as possible from the preceding one. For example, if a team has come up with five ways of raising money to make the playground more accessible, members might decide to come up with a few other ideas that have nothing to do with money (e.g., using available recycled materials to make the playground safer, motivating community members to volunteer time and effort). During brainstorming, team members can consider the facts they recorded at Stage 2 to help jog ideas (e.g., by asking, "How might this fact be diminished, eliminated, reversed, or altered to make things better?"). Note that some or even most ideas generated through brainstorming will *not* be usable, and this is OK—the main point of this stage is to loosen up thinking.

Stage 5: Solution Finding

This is the time for judging ideas critically. First, team members pinpoint the criteria they will use to identify the most promising ideas generated at Stage 4. Criteria might include whether or not ideas

- are feasible;
- are efficient and cost-effective;
- will benefit not only the specific students and situations being discussed, but others as well;
- will be accepted by everyone involved in implementing them (e.g., teachers, students, families); and

- are consistent with the values of the district, the school, and everyone involved in implementing them.

Next, team members think convergently to consider each of the best ideas from Stage 2 in light of the selected criteria. This can be done either informally, with team members keeping the criteria in the back of their minds, or more formally, with members creating a matrix, listing ideas and criteria on two axes, and employing a weighted rating system (bearing in mind that the matrix is a tool, not a formula).

Stage 6: Acceptance Finding

Team members select promising solutions and determine what they need to do to ensure that they are accepted by everyone involved, taking all the facts from Stage 2 into consideration. Discussion begins divergently, with members asking and answering *who, what, where, when, why,* and *how* questions, and ends with convergent thinking to develop a step-by-step plan of action.

Three Variations of the CPS Process for Use with Students

The CPS process is generic—anybody can use it to solve most any problem. It is particularly useful when school teams face curriculum, instruction, assessment, and discipline challenges or when they face the mismatches that inevitably occur in diverse classrooms. The three applications of the process that we discuss here—the retrofit approach to differentiated instruction, the "SODAS IF" approach, and the "Quick Brainstorm with Kids" strategy—are all meant to empower students as well as adults. The key to using CPS variations with students is trusting that they will have lots of good ideas to tap through creative problem solving.

The Retrofit Approach to Differentiated Instruction

In this iteration of the CPS process, teams work to solve a challenge related to differentiation in the classroom after it has arisen. The stages are as follows:

Stage 1: Challenge Finding. Team members notice and acknowledge the challenge.

Stage 2: Fact Finding. Team members closely examine two sets of facts: one set related to the concerns, strengths, learning styles, preferences, interests, and challenges of the student, and another related to the demands of the classroom and the curriculum.

Stage 3: Problem Finding. Team members compare the two sets of facts and identify any mismatches between them.

Stage 4: Idea Finding. Team members examine identified mismatches and brainstorm ideas for remedying them.

Stage 5: Solution Finding. Team members establish the criteria for selecting solutions that are acceptable to everyone involved.

Stage 6: Acceptance Finding. Team members select and agree to apply a solution that meets the established criteria.

To illustrate the retrofit approach in action, we offer the example of a mismatch between Shamonique, a middle school student with an IEP who requires more intensive literacy support, and the social studies class in which she has recently enrolled. Figure 4.4 shows a template that Shamonique's team used to follow the six CPS steps.

The completed template in Figure 4.4 was later shared with a group of 15 middle school students (seven of whom had IEPs) who attended an inclusive school. Figure 4.5 shows 22 ideas that these students brainstormed over the course of three minutes to solve the mismatch between Shamonique and her class. How do the students' proposed solutions compare with the ones you and your colleagues might generate? How creative, pedagogically sound, sensitive, and practical are their solutions? These students show the benefits of inclusive education!

To complete a plan for Shamonique, her team would need to select and apply criteria to the most promising solutions and prepare to ensure that the solution they finally select will be accepted by all involved. The bottom of Figure 4.4 shows the elements of Shamonique's action plan. Writing the plan out in this way helps the team to bust many of the barriers discussed

FIGURE 4.4

CPS Retrofit for Shamonique and Middle-Level Social Studies

Stage 1: Challenge Finding There is a likely mismatch between Shamonique's characteristics and the demands of her class.		**Stage 3: Problem Finding**	**Stage 4: Idea Finding**
Stage 2: Fact Finding		*Mismatches Between Shamonique and Class Demands*	*Potential Solutions (Brainstorm 2–4 per Mismatch)*
Facts About Shamonique	*Facts About Middle-Level Social Studies Class Demands*		
• Happy and enthusiastic about school and life (energetic) • Has great sense of humor • Very interested in music and musicians • Gains information from conversation and visuals • Reads using sight words; has a sight-word vocabulary of 200 words IEP Goals: • Actively engage in class using relevant comments and questions • Acquire an additional 100+ sight words • Transition in a timely manner between classes following her schedule • Learn 10+ core facts/concepts per month per academic class • Participate in co-curricular activities of her choice	• Assigned grade-level text • Teacher lectures while students take notes • Teacher is very interested in the subject matter and has a vast amount of information to share • Teacher occasionally gets off topic and goes on tangents • Limited use of visuals during lecture • Students start nightly homework in class toward the end of the period • Students randomly called upon at the start of each class to check whether homework has been read and understood • Frequent quizzes • Weekly tests on any of the information presented by the teacher in class or in the text		
Stage 5: Solution Finding (Select preferred solutions using preferred evaluation criteria)			
Evaluation Criteria: **Solutions:**			
Stage 6: Acceptance-Finding Action Plan (Who does what, when? Is the plan working?)			
Activities (List preparation and implementation steps in order)	*Success Measure and Date or Timeline*	*Responsible Person(s)*	*Outcomes*

FIGURE 4.5

22 Student Ideas to Address Mismatches for Shamonique

1. Teacher needs to stay on topic
2. Teacher could use PowerPoint presentations along with lecture (this will also help teacher stay on topic)
3. Develop a short song about the people or events being studied
4. Give her fill-in-the-blank or multiple choice tests
5. Change her homework, give her a word of the day to practice (e.g., pilgrim)
6. Ask parents to help her practice new vocabulary
7. Use vocabulary she knows for her assignments
8. Provide books with lower reading levels on the topics being studied
9. Develop jingles to help her remember what has been studied
10. Have Shamonique or other students develop the jingles
11. Teach her easy words and review them frequently
12. Do not count her weekly quiz scores toward her grade
13. Select words about music or movie stars for her to learn
14. Challenge her to improve her spelling—keep trying to find correct spelling before moving on
15. Use a computer with spelling and grammar check for work and homework
16. Use educational songs
17. Stop at times during and after lecture to have students discuss what they have heard
18. Debate frequently
19. Begin class with volunteers and then randomly select students to highlight key points after they have heard them from classmates
20. Let her make up jokes about the people being studied
21. Use graphic organizers and lecture guides
22. Present individuals who are being studied in the social studies class as pop culture figures in their time period

earlier in this chapter by holding members (responsible persons) accountable for implementing component parts of the selected solution (activities) and collecting data (success measure) in a timely fashion (date or timeline).

The SODAS IF Approach

The SODAS IF variation of the CPS process has been used successfully with students for years (Hazel, Schumaker, Sherman, & Sheldon, 1995). *SODAS* is an acronym for Situation-Options-Disadvantages-Advantages-Solution; the *IF* refers to the final stage of the process (i.e., Acceptance Finding)

- **S**ituation. Equivalent to Stage 3 (Problem Finding) of the CPS process—team members identify a specific problem
- **O**ptions. Equivalent to Stage 4 (Idea Finding)—members generate multiple ideas
- **D**isadvantages and
- **A**dvantages. Equivalent to the divergent part of Stage 5 (Solution Finding)
- **S**olution. Equivalent to the convergent part of Stage 5
- **IF**. Equivalent to Stage 6 (Acceptance Finding)

Figure 4.6 shows a template teams can use to conduct the SODAS IF variation of the CPS process.

Here's an example of how SODAS IF might work in the classroom. Ms. Quinn, a 4th grade classroom teacher, randomly draws a problem from the class-meeting suggestion box that reads, "A student calls another student's sister a name, and the students get into a shouting match in the hallway." Then, Ms. Quinn projects the SODAS IF problem-solving template onto a screen and asks her students to identify the situation using the starter phrase, "In what ways might. . . ." One student answers: "In what ways might these students identify what the real problem is and figure out how to resolve it?" Ms. Quinn sees other students nodding their heads, so she writes the question down on the template. She then asks students to break into pairs and triads and to take two minutes to generate potential solutions before sharing out to the class. A total of 12 options are generated, all of which are recorded on the template.

The next step involves identifying disadvantages for each of the 12 options. Ms. Quinn models by offering the first example and recording it on the template. Then, she asks the students to turn to a shoulder partner and discuss possible disadvantages of a different option. After a minute, she calls on various students to share what they've come up with and records their responses. She repeats this process for the remaining options, and then again to identify advantages for each of the 12 options. She directs the students to turn to different partners from last time and identify the solutions

FIGURE 4.6

The SODAS IF Problem-Solving Template with Parallel CPS Stages

SITUATION (Stage 3: Problem Finding):

____

____

____

____

OPTIONS (Stage 4: Idea Finding):

1.______	2.______	3.______

DISADVANTAGES (Stage 5: Solution Finding):

a.______	a.______	a.______
b.______	b.______	b.______
c.______	c.______	c.______
d.______	d.______	d.______

ADVANTAGES (Stage 5: Solution Finding):

a.______	a.______	a.______
b.______	b.______	b.______
c.______	c.______	c.______
d.______	d.______	d.______

SOLUTION (Stage 5: Solution Finding):

IF you agree to a solution, MAKE A PLAN (Stage 6: Acceptance Finding).
(Who will do what, when? How do you know if the plan is working?)

they think would have the most advantages and the least disadvantages. After a minute, she asks students to report out and notes their conclusions.

After everyone has shared, Ms. Quinn explains to the students that although the scenario they discussed was fictional, students in a similar situation would be expected to use the SODAS IF process to come up with solutions to their conflict, and she then asks students how the SODAS IF process might help them to solve problems in class, on the playground, with friends, and at home. She closes the lesson by sharing an example of how she herself has used the process in real life and alerting students that they will be using it to solve problems in class throughout the year.

The "Quick Brainstorm with Kids" Approach

This version of the CPS process is derived from Giangreco and colleagues (2002) and focuses students' creative thinking on brainstorming (i.e., Stage 4: Idea Finding) to solve challenges. As an example, consider a class of 1st graders who are asked to think of ways to welcome a new classmate with extensive support needs. The teacher asks them to come up with as many wild and crazy ideas as they can in three minutes or less. One student suggests that they all go to the beach together as a class; the next student piggybacks on his idea with a more realistic one: he suggests showing her how to play in the school sandbox at recess. In the end, the students come up with more than 50 ideas, most of which are actually feasible.

Focusing on What You Can Do

> *A fair idea put to use is better than a good idea kept on the polishing wheel.*
>
> —Alex Osborn (as cited in Parnes, 1992, p. 38)

Now that you have read this chapter, what have you learned about barriers to effective teaming and creative solution finding? How do you plan to use the collaboration and problem-solving tools and processes we've shared? How might you use the CPS process and its variations to expand options for meeting the needs of students and solving both large and small problems at school or elsewhere? The key is to *act,* and to get others to act as well.

References

Brandt, R. (1987). On cooperation in schools: A conversation with David and Roger Johnson. *Educational Leadership, 44*(3), 14–19.

Glasser, W. (1999). *Choice theory: A new psychology of personal freedom.* New York: Perennial.

Goleman, D., Kaufman, P., & Ray, M. (1993). *The creative spirit* [companion to PBS television series]. New York: Plume.

Hazel, H. S., Schumaker, J. E., Sherman, J. A., & Sheldon, J. (1995). *ASSET: A social skills program for adolescents.* Champaign, IL: Research Press.

Hourcade, J., & Bauwens, J. (2002). *Cooperative teaching: Rebuilding and sharing the schoolhouse.* Austin, TX: Pro-Ed.

Johnson, D. W., & Johnson, F. P. (2005). *Joining together: Group theory and skills* (9th ed.). Needham Heights, MA: Allyn & Bacon.

National Center on School Restructuring and Inclusion. (1996). *National study on inclusive education.* New York: City University of New York.

Newton, J. S., Toddy, A. W., Algozzine, B., Algozzine, K. Horner, R. H., & Cusumano, D. L. (2014). Supporting team problem solving in inclusive schools. In J. McLeskey, N. L. Waldron, F. Spooner, & B. Algozzine (Eds.), *Handbook of effective inclusive schools: Research and practice* (pp. 275–291). New York: Routledge.

Osborn, A. F. (1953/1993). *Applied imagination: Principles and procedures of creative problem solving* (3rd ed.). Amherst, MA: Creative Education Foundation Press.

Parnes, S. J. (1992a). *Source book for creative problem solving: A 50-year digest of proven innovation processes.* Amherst, MA: Creative Education Foundation Press.

Parnes, S. J. (1992b). *Visionizing: State-of-the-art processes for encouraging innovative excellence.* Amherst, MA: Creative Education Foundation Press.

Ryndak, D., Lehr, D., Ward, T., & DeBivoise, H. (2014). Collaboration and teaming in effective inclusive schools. In J. McLeskey, N. L. Waldron, F. Spooner, & B. Algozzine (Eds.), *Handbook of effective inclusive schools: Research and practice* (pp. 395–409). New York: Routledge.

Thousand, J., & Villa, R. (2000). Teaming: A powerful tool in school restructuring. In R. Villa & J. Thousand (Eds.), *Restructuring for caring and effective education: Piecing the puzzle together* (2nd ed., pp. 254–291). Baltimore: Paul H. Brookes.

Thousand, J. S., Villa, R. A., Nevin, A. I., & Paolucci-Whitcomb, P. (1995). A rationale and vision for collaborative consultation. In W. Stainback & S. Stainback (Eds.), *Controversial issues confronting special education: Divergent perspectives* (2nd ed., pp. 223–232). Baltimore: Paul H. Brookes.

Thousand, J. S., Villa, R. A., & Nevin, A. I. (2015). *Differentiating instruction: Collaborative planning and teaching for universally designed learning* (2nd ed.). Thousand Oaks, CA: Corwin.

Villa, R., & Thousand, J. (2005). *Creating an inclusive school* (2nd ed.). Alexandria, VA: ASCD.

Villa, R. A., Thousand, J. S., & Nevin, A. I. (2009). *Collaborating with students in instruction and decision making: The untapped resource.* Thousand Oaks, CA: Corwin Press.

Villa, R., Thousand, J., Nevin, A., & Meyers, H. (1996). Teacher and administrator perceptions of heterogeneous education. *Exceptional Children, 63*(1), 29–45.

CHAPTER 5

Maximizing Resources and Designing Interventions Through a Multitiered System of Supports

Jacqueline S. Thousand and Richard A. Villa

The second floor of the Schoolhouse Model (Figure II.1, p. 45) is shared by two processes intended to increase the likelihood that curriculum differentiation is successful: the Multitiered System of Supports (MTSS) and co-teaching. We will discuss co-teaching at length in Chapter 6; here, our focus is on the MTSS.

First introduced with the reauthorization of IDEIA in 2004, the MTSS is meant to prevent unnecessary special education referrals through research-based instruction in general education and swift and targeted interventions for struggling students. Originally known as Response to Intervention (or RTI), the MTSS is divided into three distinct tiers:

- Tier 1. High-quality, evidence-based core instruction in general education with frequent student progress monitoring
- Tier 2. Supplemental targeted interventions, generally delivered in small groups to students who aren't meeting expected curriculum benchmarks
- Tier 3. More intensive and individualized interventions for students who do not respond adequately to Tier 1 and 2 interventions (Villa & Thousand, 2011).

The IDEIA regulations allow for the use of an RTI process "based on a child's response to scientific research-based intervention, as a component to determine whether a child has an SLD [Specific Learning Disability]"

(California Department of Education, 2009, iii). In California, RTI has been renamed Response to Instruction and Intervention (RTI^2) to emphasize the importance of high-quality instruction in general education as the foundation for shared responsibility of student learning among all school personnel. Implementation of RTI^2 has been found to reduce disproportionate referrals for special education among certain students (e.g., English language learners, black students) (California Services for Technical Assistance and Training, 2015).

Over time, MTSS has emerged as a comprehensive system of support that strives to prevent unnecessary special education referrals and that provides schools and districts with "high-quality first instruction, supports, and interventions in academics and behavior for all students, regardless of whether they are struggling or have advanced learning needs" (California Services for Technical Assistance and Training, 2015, p. 2). The system provides an overarching organizing structure that braids RTI/RTI^2 processes together with Schoolwide Positive Behavior Support (SWPBS) systems supporting students' healthy social, emotional, and behavioral growth (Higgins Averill, & Rinaldi, 2011), and provides the framework for delivering effective instruction and behavioral supports through differentiated instruction and Universal Design for Learning principles and practices (see Chapter 7; Thousand, Villa, & Nevin, 2015).

Figure 5.1 shows a visual representation of MTSS that includes both RTI and SWPBS components. How do these two types of systems work together to create a comprehensive MTSS? In this chapter, we'll explore the answer to that question.

Response to Intervention

The RTI framework was developed in response to suspicions that providing supports for struggling students as early as possible in their schooling might reduce the number of students who end up referred to special education. Representing the academic side of the MTSS pyramid shown in Figure 5.1, RTI integrates resources from general education, special education, and other programs, such as those for English language learners,

FIGURE 5.1

The MTSS Pyramid

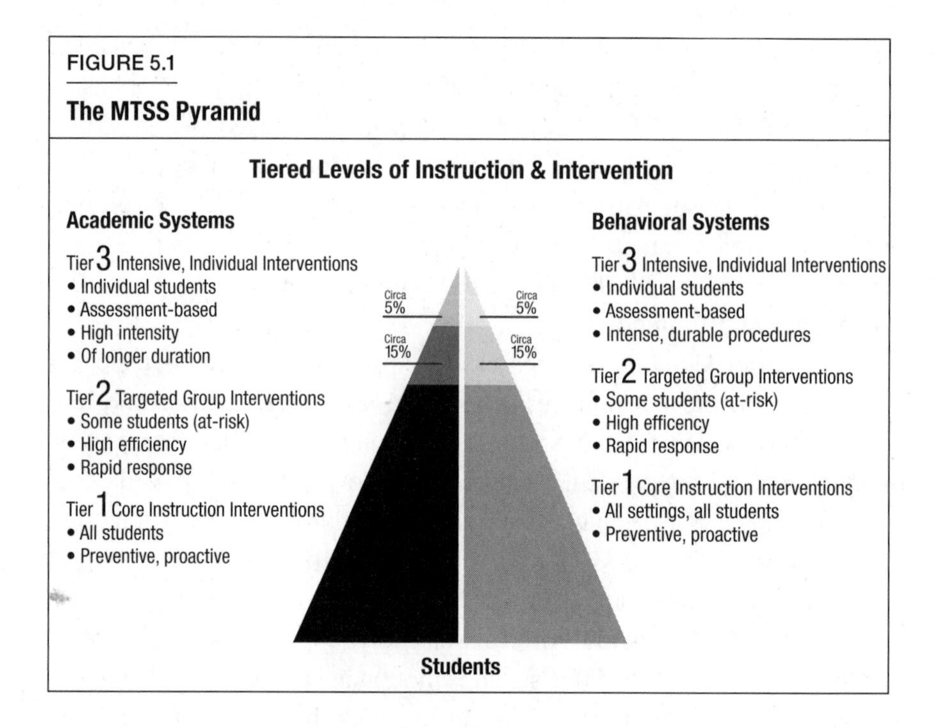

into a comprehensive system for quickly responding to students who are struggling with the general education curriculum. Figure 5.2 shows the key elements of a successful RTI process. The three tiers of RTI are as follows:

- Tier 1. This tier involves regular (e.g., three times per year) schoolwide screening of all students' progress in the general education curriculum as well as classroom-based instruction and individualized and group interventions that represent the core instructional program. Using research-based methods proven to be effective with a wide range of diverse learners (see Chapter 7), teachers should be able to ensure that 80 to 90 percent of students meet predetermined benchmarks in expected time frames. When general educators co-teach with support specialists, differentiation is especially effective, as the adults are able to mesh their separate spheres of knowledge and skills in any number of ways (e.g., regarding content, instruction, use of technology or materials, human relations and motivation, and collaborative planning and problem solving).

FIGURE 5.2

Key RTI Elements

1. Belief that every child can and does learn
2. Acknowledgment that a learning difficulty may lie in a "mismatch" between student characteristics and the teaching/learning environment
3. Early and swift intervention versus a "wait to fail" approach
4. Services come to a student without the student being labeled or made eligible for special education
5. Regular, periodic (e.g., three times per year) 'universal' screening of the entire school population
6. Proactive, high-quality evidenced-based instruction in general education classrooms
7. Regular team meetings to examine data and collaboratively problem solve (using an established solution-finding method such as those described in Chapter 4)
8. Data-based decision making by teams to determine appropriate interventions
9. Supplemental high-quality instruction by classroom teachers and specialists matched to student strengths and needs
10. Research-based interventions provided at increasing levels of intensity
11. Continuous progress monitoring during interventions
12. Fluid and flexible grouping of students for instruction, remediation, and enrichment
13. Monitoring of instructional and intervention group composition to assure membership does not remain static and result in de facto tracking
14. Active family involvement in decision making, with families being informed of student progress in their native language or preferred mode of communication
15. Can replace the "IQ-achievement discrepancy model" to identify a specific learning disability via documentation of a student having received research-based instruction and increasingly intensified interventions and having failed to respond to them

- Tier 2. This tier is designed to address the approximately 15 percent of students who fail to meet expected benchmarks in Tier 1. Tier 2 interventions are specifically designed to address identified areas of concern (e.g., decoding, reading fluency). Instruction in this tier is typically delivered to small groups of three to six students with similar learning needs during a separate 30-minute session each day. Student progress is monitored much more frequently in Tier 2 in than in Tier 1—every two to four weeks. Interventions may last from several weeks to an entire academic year.

  In Tier 2, co-teachers engage in "parallel co-teaching" (see Chapter 6) to teach both the general group as well as subgroups of students who require specific interventions at the same time. Optimally, the general education classroom will be divided into three or four stations, with each focused on a different kind of learning. Placement in these groups should be based on students' immediate instructional needs rather than on any labels or categorizations.

- Tier 3. The interventions in this tier are designed to address the 5 percent or so of students who were unable to make progress despite the supports offered in the other two tiers. Educators offer longer and more frequent interventions to students who need them at this point, and administer them either individually or in groups of two or three. Interventions in Tier 3 span over weeks and months to ensure positive outcomes.

  It is important to note that interventions in Tier 3 *do not* mean that affected students should automatically be assessed for placement in special education. However, if interventions at this stage still prove ineffective, such assessment may be considered as part of a deeper examination of the students' overall health, including vision, hearing, social/emotional and language development, and information processing skills. As in Tier 2, interventions here rely upon parallel co-teaching among the broad range of school personnel who share responsibility for each student's success.

Positive Behavior Support

Students who display behaviors that educators consider challenging risk facing many undesirable outcomes, including being removed from the general education environment, losing relationships with peers, and experiencing negative interventions (e.g., use of psychotropic drugs, punishment responses); positive behavior support (PBS) exists to minimize and prevent behaviors that might lead to these kinds of consequences. It begins with setting both schoolwide and individual behavioral expectations for students and rewarding those who meet them. Students with more frequent or intensive disruptive behaviors receive individualized support via direct instruction on impulse control, problem solving, and social skills; contracts, daily check-in and check-out systems, and daily progress reports; and frequent praise and rewards for achieving goals. In addition to helping keep students with behavioral challenges in the general education environment, PBS is meant to help students enhance their quality of life more generally.

A Schoolwide Positive Behavior Support System

A Schoolwide Positive Behavior Support (SWPBS) system represents the behavioral side of the MTSS shown in Figure 5.1. Implementing such a system requires educators to embrace inclusive values and practices and to construct a culture of competence where teaching, monitoring, and rewarding rule-following behavior are the norm. A SWPBS system requires educators to work with rather than send away students who pose behavioral challenges —to examine why students are acting out, what function their behavior serves, what need their behavior is, or is not, meeting. It also requires educators to collect data to determine the effects of behavioral interventions.

Figure 5.3 identifies six best practices for guiding school personnel to effectively implement a SWPBS system.

As with RTI, SWPBS is divided into three tiers:

- Tier 1. In this tier, behavioral supports are universal and address the needs of the majority of students. Supports here include defining and teaching schoolwide behavioral expectations, establishing systems for recognizing and celebrating norm-following behavior, and collecting data (e.g., office discipline referrals, teacher-generated requests for assistance) to assess the effects of the SWPBS system on overall student behaviors and to identify students who may need additional help.
- Tier 2. The supports in this tier are for the 10 to 15 percent of students who the data reveal more frequently or seriously violate behavioral norms and who can benefit from more explicit supports such as individualized behavior contracts, self-management strategies (e.g., identifying emotional triggers, using calming techniques), adult or peer mentoring, and a daily check-in and check-out system (Crone,

FIGURE 5.3

Schoolwide Positive Behavior Support (SWPBS) Best Practices

1. The school has a well-articulated SWPBS system that is part of the school's MTSS and that complements the RTI approach to supporting academic and behavioral/social learning.
2. Teachers and other school staff receive quality training in positive behavioral support approaches and methods for managing medical or behavioral emergencies.
3. School staff deliberately and routinely use positive behavioral supports to promote a sense of community and safety for all students.
4. Teachers and other school personnel understand and believe that behavior is a form of communication, often about unmet needs.
5. When a student shows recurring or intensified disruptive behavior, a team approach is taken to determine the function of the behavior in order to develop comprehensive interventions and supports rather than seeking special education eligibility or placing the student in a more restrictive setting outside of the general education classroom.
6. A safe and ethical crisis and emergency response intervention is developed to support students whose behaviors may escalate and pose a danger to themselves or others.

Hawken, & Horner, 2015). Some Tier 2 supports can benefit many if not all students in a classroom and may be used in Tier 1 as well.

- Tier 3. Supports in Tier 3 address the needs of the 5 percent or fewer of students who exhibit behaviors that are frequent, intensive, persistent, severely challenging (e.g., causing harm to self or others), and disruptive to learning. These students need intensive, individualized supports that are clearly articulated in a positive behavior intervention plan (BIP). Developing a BIP requires a team (including the student, whenever possible) to examine what function the challenging behavior serves for the student and why it is recurring (Villa, Thousand, & Nevin, 2010). This process is known as a functional behavioral assessment, or FBA (O'Neill & Jameson, 2016). Is the student trying to gain attention? Does the behavior indicate boredom or a need to expend energy? Is it an attempt to avoid or escape a situation? Is it due to poor impulse control? The team arrives at a hypothesis based on observations of and interviews with the student and those who know him or her in multiple contexts (e.g., teachers, parents, peers).

At its essence, a positive BIP is a teaching plan that specifies what the student, teachers, and others will do to alter the environment and reinforce positive behaviors to supplant the challenging ones. (For more information on the specifics of positive behavior interventions, see the *Journal of Positive Behavior Interventions*, available online at pbi.sagepub.com.)

Commonalities and Differences among MTSS, RTI, and SWPBS

Both RTI and SWPBS originated as tiered support structures for individual students. The purpose of MTSS is to unify those two structures through shared ownership and collaborative planning and teaching. In addition, MTSS is aimed at activating districtwide alignment of resources and partnerships (e.g., social services, continuing education, juvenile justice) to achieve high expectations for *all* students, including high achievers, rather than only for the 10 to 15 percent who might require intensive interventions. The MTSS approach requires educators to learn and use positive behavior support approaches as well as Universal Design for Learning principles to differentiate learning for all students.

All three structures

- are based on a *vision* that all students, regardless of their backgrounds or challenges, *can and do learn*;
- use a *collaborative approach* and well-defined *problem-solving processes* to identify challenges, develop interventions, and evaluate the effectiveness of interventions in a multitiered system of services;
- employ research-based academic and behavioral instruction that is *culturally and linguistically relevant* in Tier 1 and appropriate research-based interventions for improving outcomes at Tiers 2 and 3; and
- rely on *data collection and assessment systems* (e.g., universal screening, diagnostics, progress monitoring) to inform decisions regarding each tier of service.

These common features are brought together in the seven-stage decision-making cycle shown in Figure 5.4, which is driven by ongoing monitoring of student progress and data-based collaborative problem solving. The

FIGURE 5.4

MTSS Decision-Making Cycle

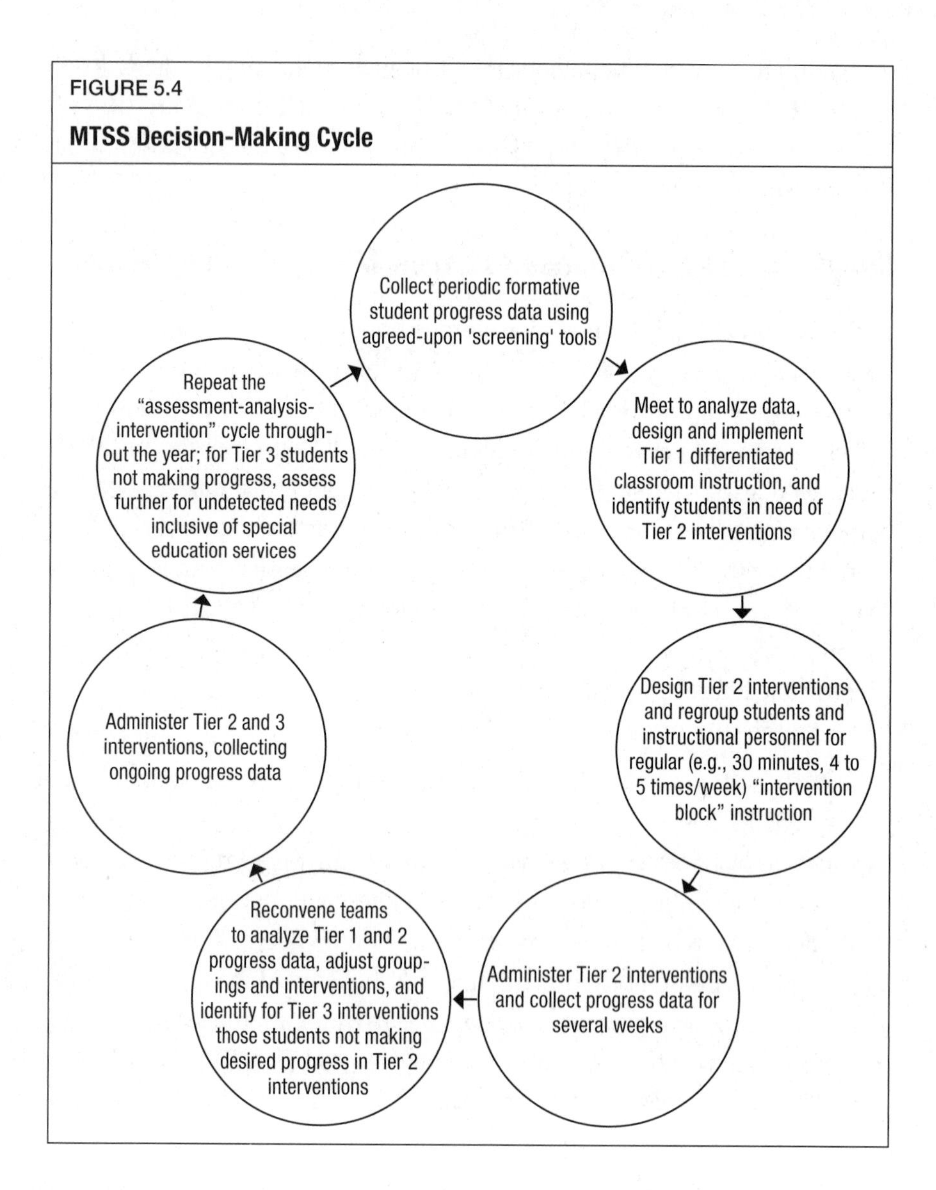

collaborative strategies and creative problem-solving processes discussed in Chapter 4 can be used at each stage of the cycle; for example, teams might use the structured agenda format shown in Figure 4.2 (p. 80) to better meet goals, make meetings more effective, and communicate more clearly with other team members.

Figure 5.5 shows the agenda and minutes of a primary grade-level core MTSS team's initial planning meeting for the school year. Note that co-teaching is one of the Tier 1 supports the team uses and that no time is wasted determining the intervention strategies for Tiers 2 and 3. Also note that academic, behavior, and English development specialists are included in the core team to address issues on both the academic and behavior sides of the school's MTSS. (In Chapter 6, we'll further discuss co-teaching as a process for integrating human resources to strengthen a comprehensive MTSS.)

FIGURE 5.5

Sample Agenda for Core Primary-Grade MTSS Team's Initial Meeting of the Year

People present:	**Absentees:**	**Others who need to know:**
Eli (VP & MTSS Coordinator)	______	Chris (Principal)
Miki (Grade 2 Teacher)	______	Deshon (Paraeducator)
Elise (Multi-Age 1/2 Teacher)	______	
Nadine (Special Educator)		
Ann (Literacy Coach)		
Ricardo (Behavioral Specialist)		
Suyapa (ELL Teacher)		
Antoine (Grade 3 Teacher)		

Roles:	**This Meeting**	**Next Meeting**
Timekeeper:	Ann	Ricardo
Recorder:	Suyapa	Antoine
Encourager:	Nadine	Miki
Jargon Buster:	Eli	Elise

Meeting Agenda for September 13th

Agenda Items	**Time Limits**
1. Positive comments and agenda review	2 minutes
2. Review formative student assessment data	10 minutes
3. Assign Tier 1 co-teachers	4 minutes
4. Solicit input on draft differentiated co-taught unit plan	12 minutes
5. Pause for group processing of progress toward task accomplishment and use of interpersonal skills	3 minutes
6. Establish Tier 2 and 3 Intervention teaching teams	5 minutes
7. Select research-based intervention strategies	9 minutes
8. Agree upon progress monitoring strategies, roles, timeline, and schedule	10 minutes
9. Final group processing of task and relationship	5 minutes
Total Time:	60 minutes

continued

FIGURE 5.5 *(continued)*

Sample Agenda for Core Primary-Grade MTSS Team's Initial Meeting of the Year

Minutes of Outcomes

Action Items	**Person(s) Responsible**	**By When?**
1. Communicate outcomes to absentees	Nadine	Sept. 14
2. Complete co-teaching unit plan	Ann/Miki/Elise	Sept. 15
3. Inform parents of Tier 2 intervention groups	Eli/Ann	Sept. 14
4. Assess progress of assigned students	All	Sept. 27

Agenda Building for Next Meeting

Date: September 27th **Time:** 12:15–1:30 PM **Location:** Conference Room

References

California Department of Education. (2009). *Determining specific learning disability eligibility using Response to Instruction and Intervention (RTI²)*. Sacramento, CA: Author.

California Services for Technical Assistance and Training. (2015). A multitiered system of supports with response to intervention and universal design for learning: Putting it all together (Special insert). *The Special EDge, 28*(2), 1–4.

California Statewide Task Force on Special Education. (2015, March). *One system: Reforming education to serve all students*. Sacramento, CA: California Department of Education.

Crone, D. A., Hawken, L. S., & Horner, R. H. (2015). *Responding to problem behavior in schools: The Behavior Education Program* (2nd ed.). New York: Guilford.

Higgins Averill, O., & Rinaldi, C. (2011, May). *Research brief: Multitier system of supports* (MTSS). Waltham, MA: Urban Special Education Leadership Collaborative. Retrieved from www.urbancollaborative.org/research-briefs.

Shogren, K., McCart, A., Lyon, K., & Sailor, W. (2015). All means all: Building knowledge for inclusive schoolwide transformation. *Research and Practice for Persons with Severe Disabilities, 40*(3), 173–192.

Thousand, J. S., Villa, R. A., & Nevin, A. I. (2015). *Differentiating instruction: Planning for universal design and teaching for college and career readiness* (2nd ed.). Thousand Oaks, CA: Corwin.

Villa, R. A., & Thousand, J. S. (2011). *RTI: Co-teaching and differentiated instruction*. Port Chester, NY: National Professional Resources.

Villa, R. A., & Thousand, J. S. (2016). *The inclusive education checklist: A self-assessment of quality inclusive education practices*. Naples, FL: National Professional Resources.

Villa, R. A., Thousand, J. S., & Nevin, A. I. (2010). *Collaborating with students in instruction and decision making: The untapped resource*. Thousand Oaks, CA: Corwin.

CHAPTER 6

Co-Teaching to Promote Student Access and Success

Richard A. Villa and Jacqueline S. Thousand

Co-teaching is an arrangement of two or more members of the school community who distribute planning, instructional, and assessment responsibilities for students in mixed-ability classrooms among themselves regularly and for an extended period. By jigsawing the unique instructional expertise, curriculum knowledge, and personal interests of educators and specialists, co-teaching teams bring a richer learning experience to all students, a higher teacher-to-student ratio, enhanced problem-solving capacity, and more immediate and accurate diagnoses of student needs (Nevin, Thousand, & Villa, 2009; Villa, Thousand, & Nevin, 2013). Co-teaching offers a legal, cost-effective way to partner general educators (i.e., masters of content) with special educators and other specialists (i.e., masters of access), increasing the likelihood that students with diverse learning profiles will succeed in the general education curriculum.

The most common type of co-teaching partnership involves a general educator co-teaching with a special educator, but anyone can take part: reading specialists, math coaches, librarians, English language learning specialists, speech and language pathologists, occupational or physical therapists, teachers of students identified as gifted and talented, teacher librarians, psychologists, counselors, administrators, university personnel, paraeducators, parents, business or other community volunteers, and even students themselves (Nevin et al., 2009; Villa, Thousand, & Nevin, 2010; Villa et al., 2013).

It is possible for paraeducators to provide meaningful instruction in all co-teaching approaches. However, it will require planning time and careful training and supervision for complementary and team co-teaching. It's also worth noting that students who practice some semblance of co-teaching —whether actually co-teaching a class with an adult or through peer tutoring, cooperative group learning, or dialogue teaching—are more likely to increase their academic achievement and to collaborate with others and advocate for themselves effectively as adults (Villa et al., 2010). We have worked with schools to establish programs where up to 100 students are trained to serve as same- or cross-aged tutors, and we've helped high schools establish student-adult co-teaching teams that earn school credit for the student co-teachers. In establishing both types of programs, staff must pay special attention to recruiting, training, and supervising participating students.

The Four Main Co-Teaching Approaches

In a comprehensive national survey, teachers of diverse classrooms reported using four main co-teaching approaches: supportive, parallel, complementary, and team (National Center on Educational Restructuring and Inclusion, 1995). None of these approaches is better than another; the goal of all four is to marshal additional human resources to support student learning. Many teachers who are new to collaborating on instruction in the classroom begin with the supportive co-teaching approach because it involves less planning and coordination with co-teachers. As co-teaching skills and relationships strengthen, educators move on to engage in the other three approaches.

Supportive Co-Teaching

In this approach, one co-teacher takes the lead instructional role and the other rotates among students providing a variety of supports. The co-teacher in the supportive role may watch or listen as students work together and provide one-to-one academic, behavioral, or communication support when necessary while the other teacher continues to direct the lesson. The supportive co-teacher can also gather diagnostic information by observing and closely monitoring students. There can be more than one co-teacher in the supportive role.

Supportive co-teaching increases the ratio of adults to students, with both teachers sharing responsibility for all the students in the classroom. Students often express appreciation for the extra help that having two or more co-teachers affords. However, co-teachers in the supportive role must ensure that they don't become overly focused on a handful of students, hovering over them and blocking their interactions with others, as this can alienate the rest of the class. It's possible and even advisable for co-teachers to rotate between lead and support functions, lest co-teachers who don't get the opportunity to lead instruction become frustrated and resentful.

Parallel Co-Teaching

Parallel co-teaching is when two or more people work with different groups of students in different sections of the classroom at the same time. This is the only one of the four co-teaching approaches that does not involve large-group instruction. Although co-teachers share responsibility for planning for all students in the classroom, each of them instructs or monitors one subgroup. Co-teachers may rotate among the groups, and groups may sometimes work without a co-teacher for at least part of the time. As Figure 6.1 shows, there are many variations of parallel co-teaching, making it a versatile way to differentiate instruction. Parallel co-teachers can differentiate what they do with each group, thus affording students multiple options for accessing and interacting with content in ways that match their particular learning preferences, styles, and needs.

Parallel co-teachers must guard against creating a special class-within-the-class by routinely grouping low-performing students together and having the same co-teacher work with them at all times (as such configurations have been found to result in lower student achievement and to stigmatize both the students and the co-teacher instructing the group [Marzano, Pickering, & Pollack, 2001]). All co-teachers should work with all groups so that students can benefit from their different approaches and expertise. Further, groupings should be fluid, flexible, and, for the most part, heterogeneous so that students can interact with and learn from classmates with

FIGURE 6.1

Variations of Parallel Co-Teaching

Split Class
Each co-teacher is responsible for a particular group of students, monitoring understanding of a lesson, providing guided instruction, or re-teaching the group if necessary.

Learning Centers or Stations
Each co-teacher is responsible for guiding instruction at a center or station. Students or co-teachers may rotate.

Lab or Cooperative Group Monitoring
Each co-teacher takes responsibility for monitoring, data collection, and providing feedback and assistance to a given number of lab or cooperative groups of students.

Learning Style Focus
One co-teacher works with a group of students emphasizing visual strategies, while another emphasizes auditory strategies, and yet another emphasizes kinesthetic strategies. Students can experience one or all learning styles. When rotating students among the learning styles, students start with the one most closely matched to their strengths and interests to spark motivation and increase the likelihood of academic success.

Supplementary Instruction
One co-teacher works with the class on a concept, skill, or learning strategy while the other (a) provides extra guidance to students self-identified or teacher-identified as needing extra assistance; (b) instructs a targeted group to apply or generalize the concept, skill, or strategy; or (c) provides enrichment and extension experiences.

different skills and perspectives. The exception to this is in the second and third tiers of MTSS delivery, where students are deliberately grouped homogeneously for a specific purpose and for a limited time period. In these cases, parallel co-teachers still share responsibility for all students and, over time, instruct them all regardless of how they're grouped.

Complementary Co-Teaching

In this approach, one co-teacher does something to enhance, supplement, or otherwise add value to another's instruction. For example, one co-teacher might provide a lecture on the content while the other paraphrases statements and models note taking. Other examples of complementary co-teaching strategies include preteaching idioms and figurative language, creating visual supports or charts of key vocabulary terms, introducing learning tools such as sentence frames and anchor charts, providing examples or analogies, and checking for understanding. As in the other co-teaching approaches, complementary co-teachers share responsibility for all of the students in the classroom. They can exchange lead and complementary roles at various times during lessons as well as over time as they become more proficient with one another's content. All members of a complementary co-teaching team contribute to the quality of instruction by sharing their unique expertise, talents, and interests, and may end up incorporating strategies learned from their co-teachers into their own instructional repertoires.

Because complementary co-teachers are both teaching the whole class at the same time, it is critical that they take care not to repeat themselves too much or to neglect monitoring student interactions. Often, there will be a gap in content expertise between co-teachers (especially between special educators or support specialists and content-area teachers), but this isn't necessarily a drawback if they all have something to offer: speech and language pathologists have expertise in communication, for example, and special educators have expertise in adapting curriculum and specialized learning strategies. A paraeducator may speak fluent Spanish, or perhaps one co-teacher is especially skilled at creating graphic organizers. By planning and teaching together, all members of a complementary co-teaching team have an opportunity to acquire new skills.

Team Co-Teaching

During team co-teaching, two or more people do what traditionally was done solely by the individual classroom teacher: plan, teach, assess, and assume responsibility for all of the students in the classroom. In an effective team co-teaching relationship, co-teachers can practically finish one another's sentences. Team co-teachers jointly decide who does what before, during, and after the lesson, ensuring that their work is more-or-less equally divided. They simultaneously deliver content and facilitate access to it.

In the team approach, co-teachers might alternate explaining the steps of a procedure to students during a lesson; prior to a lesson, they might role-play how they want students to interact during an activity or discuss how they'll work together to solve a content-related or behavioral problem. The advantages of team co-teaching are similar to those of the complementary approach, with each team member contributing according to his or her strengths. For example, in a science class, a co-teacher with an interest in history might explain how certain inventions affected society, or one with a mechanical bent might explain how the inventions actually worked. As with complementary co-teaching, team co-teachers must guard against neglecting to closely monitor students or dominating the class period with teacher talk.

Best Practices for Effective Co-Teaching: Role Release

To move from supportive (which least capitalizes upon all team members' skills) to parallel to complementary to team co-teaching, co-teachers must trust one another enough to release their expertise to and exchange roles with their partners. This phenomenon is known as *role release* and is one hallmark of any effective co-teaching relationship. Another hallmark is the ability to move in and out of the four approaches depending on the demands of the content and the needs of students. For co-teachers to do this, they must push against the natural tendency to stay within their comfort zones. The truest test of effective co-teaching is whether all students in the class view both co-teachers as their legitimate teachers.

A Co-Teaching Planning Form to Guide Instruction

Planning provides co-teachers with a shared understanding of the curriculum, language, and social-skill content of a lesson, allows them to determine what their specific co-teaching roles will be, and increases the likelihood that they will execute their responsibilities effectively, be clear on expected student outcomes, and be able to make adjustments for necessary differentiation during class.

To help co-teachers plan collaboratively, we offer the Co-Teaching Planning Form in Figure 6.2. The form first prompts co-teachers to consider content and assessment dimensions: the curriculum standards to be addressed, the materials and room arrangement necessary to facilitate learning, and the method of assessing students' performance. Next, co-teachers are prompted to think about what they each need to *do* before, during, and after instruction. For each time block, co-teachers

- discuss and agree upon the content objectives and the instructional processes that they intend to use;
- consider their students' learning differences and plan for differentiation of materials, objectives, instruction, and assessments;
- select the co-teaching approach or approaches that they believe will be the best fit; and
- identify and differentiate what they each will do in their respective co-teaching roles.

The final question on the form prompts co-teachers to identify where, when, and how they will debrief and evaluate student outcomes. This question prompts co-teachers to engage in the recursive cycle of planning, teaching, and reflective analysis, which promotes effective instruction.

Figure 6.3 shows how a 6th grade co-teaching team composed of a math teacher and a special educator completed the form. As you can see, they agreed to use supportive, parallel, and complementary co-teaching approaches to structure a lesson on the concept of absolute value with their 38 students who spoke six different primary languages. Of these 38 students, seven were eligible for special education.

Planning for Professional Growth and Future Partnerships

Anyone involved in teaching for any length of time knows about the importance of educators being *reflective practitioners* who strive to improve their practice by assessing student performance and soliciting feedback on their own performance from colleagues. They reflect on these assessment data and feedback to make better decisions in future lessons and to arrange for additional training, coaching, or mentoring. Co-teachers are in an ideal situation to spur their own professional growth through dialogue with their classroom teaching partners, with whom they can collaborate on setting professional goals and who can provide them with immediate support and encouragement.

FIGURE 6.2

Co-Teaching Planning Form

Date: ______________ Co-Teachers: ____

What *curriculum standard*(s) is/are addressed?
What *materials* do co-teachers and students need?
What is the *room arrangement*? Is space outside the class used? (Draw a picture.)
How is student *learning assessed*?

What does each co-teacher do before, during, and after the lesson?

Co-Teachers			Name:	Name:	Name:
What are tasks I need to do *before* instruction?					
For each of the following instructional time blocks, what are we doing *during* instruction?					
Content and Process: What are we teaching? How are we teaching to it?	*Differentiation:* What learning differences do students have? How do we differentiate?	*Co-Teaching:* Which co-teaching approach(es) will we use?	What will I be doing during this time block?	What will I be doing during this time block?	What will I be doing during this time block?
		Supportive Parallel Complementary Team			
		Supportive Parallel Complementary Team			
		Supportive Parallel Complementary Team			
What are tasks I need to do *after* instruction?					
Where, when, and how do co-teachers debrief and evaluate the outcomes of instruction?					

FIGURE 6.3

Example of Co-Teaching Planning Form Used by a 6th Grade Co-Teaching Team

Date: November 1 Co-Teachers: Steve (Middle-Level Math Educator) Jodi (Special Educator)

What curriculum standard(s) is/are addressed? Common Core Math 6.NS: The Number System: Apply and extend previous understandings of numbers to the system of rational numbers.

What *materials* do the co-teachers and students need? Students: Number lines and number-line strips at tables, texts at tables, a problem worksheet per student; Teachers: Whiteboard, markers

What is the *room arrangement*? Table clusters of four to five (no space outside of classroom is used)

How is student *learning assessed*? 1) Questioning during instruction, application, and closure; 2) exit-pass response to question; 3) homework to be checked at entry the following day

What does each co-teacher do before, during, and after the lesson?

Co-Teachers			Name: Steve	Name: Jodi
What are tasks I need to do *before* instruction?			I prepare first draft of materials; adapt with Jodi	I adapt first draft of materials with Steve
For each of the following instructional time blocks, what are we doing *during* instruction?				
Content and Process: What are we teaching? How are we teaching to it?	*Differentiation:* What learning differences do students have? How do we differentiate?	*Co-Teaching:* Which co-teaching approach(es) will we use?	What will I be doing during this time block?	What will I be doing during this time block?
Objective: Apply understanding of absolute value as the distance from zero on the number line. Processes: Direct instruction, modeling, cooperative group guided practice; exit-pass check for understanding	Several students are easily distracted; clarification and redirection support provided	**Supportive** Parallel Complementary Team	I lead review and correction of homework, clarify and re-teach, as needed	I monitor via proximal control, prompt attention and correction of errors
	Several students need and provided manipulatives to support construct understanding	Supportive Parallel **Complementary** Team	I lead instruction and questioning and set up application practice	I complement with math language and examples modeled and written on the whiteboard
	Cooperative group application with manipulatives (at all tables) for targeted student support	Supportive **Parallel** Complementary Team	I monitor groups that include students using number line strip manipulatives to determine absolute value.	I monitor other groups' practicing application problems (with number lines provided on each table as a support)

FIGURE 6.3 *(continued)*

Example of Co-Teaching Planning Form Used by a 6th Grade Co-Teaching Team

What are tasks I need to do *after* instruction?	We jointly analyze exit pass and homework	We jointly analyze exit pass and homework
Where, when, and how do co-teachers debrief and evaluate the outcomes of instruction?		
Daily 20-minute planning session during share preparation period		

Co-teachers need to know what is expected of them if they are to accurately self-assess and reflect on their co-teaching practice. To this end, we have created the 28-item Co-Teacher Self-Assessment Form (see Figure 6.4). Co-teachers can rate the 28 items individually and then compare ratings with their partner or partners, discussing their strengths and identifying areas for improvement. Anyone responsible for observing co-teachers can use the checklist to provide constructive feedback, which can lead to professional reflection and growth.

FIGURE 6.4

Are We Really a Co-Teaching Team? Self-Assessment Form

Directions: Using the 5-point scale, circle the number that best represents the degree to which you agree with each statement. Use your results to set goals!

5 - Always; 4 - Usually; 3 - Sometimes; 2 - Rarely; 1 - Never

Culture of Collaboration

5 4 3 2 1 We value modeling collaboration and teamwork for our students.
5 4 3 2 1 We identify the resources and talents of each co-teacher.
5 4 3 2 1 We share ideas, information, and materials.
5 4 3 2 1 We are aware of and depend on one another to follow through on tasks and responsibilities even when we are not directly in one another's presence.
5 4 3 2 1 We freely communicate our questions and concerns with one another.
5 4 3 2 1 We have a process for resolving our disagreements and use it when faced with problems and conflicts.
5 4 3 2 1 We celebrate the process as well as outcomes and successes of co-teaching.

Planning

5 4 3 2 1	We have regularly scheduled times to meet and discuss our work.
5 4 3 2 1	We identify student strengths and needs and use this information in planning.
5 4 3 2 1	We agree on the curriculum standards that will be addressed in our instruction.
5 4 3 2 1	We agree on and share responsibility for deciding what to teach (i.e., the instructional content and curriculum standards).
5 4 3 2 1	We share responsibility for deciding how to teach (i.e., the instructional process).
5 4 3 2 1	We share responsibility for deciding how to assess student learning (i.e., the student products and our assessments).
5 4 3 2 1	We share responsibility for differentiating content, instruction, and assessment.
5 4 3 2 1	We share responsibility for deciding which co-teaching approach(es) we will use and who teaches what part of a lesson based upon content demands, our expertise, and the needs of and benefits to the students.

Implementation

5 4 3 2 1	We use a variety of co-teaching approaches.
5 4 3 2 1	We effectively implement the co-teaching approach(es) we've planned to use.
5 4 3 2 1	We are flexible and make changes as needed during instruction.
5 4 3 2 1	We ensure that each co-teacher teaches each student at some time.
5 4 3 2 1	We carry out discipline norms and procedures we jointly agreed upon.
5 4 3 2 1	We have fun with the students and each other when we co-teach.
5 4 3 2 1	We are both viewed by our students as their teachers.

Reflection

5 4 3 2 1	We provide one another feedback on the effectiveness of our co-teaching.
5 4 3 2 1	We plan for improvements in our instruction based upon assessed student performance and our reflection.
5 4 3 2 1	We assess, discuss, and celebrate our own growth in co-teaching together.

Promoting Co-Teaching

5 4 3 2 1	We seek and enjoy additional professional development to be better co-teachers.
5 4 3 2 1	We provide mentorship to others who want to co-teach or are new at co-teaching.
5 4 3 2 1	We communicate our need for logistical support and resources.

Final Thoughts

Though co-teaching isn't required for differentiating instruction, it is a potentially powerful way to maximize the *mindware* of human resources in schools (Bauwens & Mueller, 2000). The presence of a diversity of teachers in the classroom and the exchange of ideas, knowledge, and skills among them work to ensure that differentiation will succeed.

References

Bauwens, J., & Mueller, P. H. (2000). Maximizing the mindware of human resources. In R. A. Villa & J. S. Thousand (Eds.), *Restructuring for caring and effective education: Piecing the puzzle together* (2nd ed., pp. 328–359). Baltimore: Paul H. Brookes.

Marzano, R., Pickering, D., & Pollock, J. (2001). *Classroom instruction that works: Research-based strategies for increasing student achievement.* Alexandria, VA: ASCD.

National Center on Educational Restructuring and Inclusion. (1995). *National study on inclusion: Overview and summary report.* New York: City University of New York Graduate School and University Center.

Nevin, A., Thousand, J., & Villa, R. (2009). *A guide to co-teaching with paraeducators: Practical tips for educators.* Thousand Oaks, CA: Corwin.

Villa, R. A., Thousand, J. S., & Nevin, A. I. (2010). *Collaborating with students in instruction and decision making: The untapped resource.* Thousand Oaks, CA: Corwin.

Villa, R. A., Thousand, J. S., & Nevin, A. I. (2013). *A guide to co-teaching: New lessons and strategies to facilitate student learning* (3rd ed.). Thousand Oaks, CA: Corwin.

CHAPTER 7

Differentiated Instruction: Access to the General Education Curriculum for All

Jacqueline S. Thousand, Alice Udvari-Solner, and Richard A. Villa

Let's get to know three students in Ms. Chavez's 12th grade history class at Monarch High School—Alcides, Heydar, and Christina. Alcides seems to succeed effortlessly in both academics and extracurricular activities. He is the captain of the soccer team, he plays tennis, and he plays first trumpet in the high school band. Passionate about environmental issues, Alcides volunteers his opinions with confidence in public settings. He is also opinionated about school politics and was elected by his peers as their representative to the school board. Alcides exhausted the high school math curriculum and is taking advanced math classes at the university in the evening. Statistics, data analysis, technology applications, and Internet research are strong skill areas. He was recently instrumental in updating the school website to make it more navigable and user-friendly. Alcides has shown ability in teaching others but admittedly does not like working in groups because he believes they represent "communism in disguise."

Heydar arrived from Libya, where his family was killed in the Libyan civil war. Catholic Charities assisted him in coming to the United States to live with his uncle, who is also a relative newcomer to this country, and who recently lost his job. Heydar and his uncle are temporarily residing in a homeless shelter. Heydar is learning English. Very motivated to communicate and use his emerging English, he seeks out classmates with his approachable smile, curious disposition, and cooperative and friendly manner. Heydar shows talent with graphic arts and uses comical drawings to communicate his ideas when words fail. He often carries a prized old digital camera and pictures of his life in Libya as a social bridge to initiate conversations with others. Heydar's teachers have noticed his interest in anything mechanical and his ability to solve technological problems by taking things apart. The art teacher has noticed his eye for detail and has taken him under her wing to create a mural in the cafeteria. Two paraeducators in the school speak Arabic and, along with Heydar's uncle, help translate for Heydar. Because of his unstable housing, Heydar frequently comes to school tired and has fallen asleep several times in his classes.

Christina enjoys everything about being a 12th grader. Approaching each class with enthusiasm, she is known for her sense of humor and physical energy. Well liked by male and female friends, she has been described as empathetic in her relationships. Because of her limited sight word and academic vocabulary, one of her continuing challenges at the secondary level has been to access and gain meaning through text. She learns significantly from conversations and visual presentations. Christina has Down syndrome and is eligible for special education services. The goals in her IEP offer insight into her educational priorities: actively engaging in class discussions and small-group work by making relevant comments or asking questions; writing short paragaphs with support from peers and technology; making timely transition between classes by independently following a schedule; participating in extracurricular activities of her choice; developing work skills through community job placements; and walking or taking public transportation independently in the community.

A diverse classroom composition is not unusual; in fact, it is the norm in today's multicultural and multilingual inclusive schools. In this chapter, we'll examine the tools and strategies that Ms. Chavez can use to ensure that all 28 of her students successfully engage with the curriculum in her history class.

Access to Curriculum and Differented Instruction Through Retrofit and Universal Design for Learning Approaches

The Individual with Disabilities Education Improvement Act (IDEIA) of 2004 requires students with disabilities to have the opportunity to participate in the same general education curriculum taught to all other students—what the *Federal Register* defines as the "curriculum that is used with nondisabled children" (1999, p. 1470). The general education curriculum refers to the whole educational experience, not just to curricular content; it includes all of the processes and products associated with curriculum delivery and guarantees access to instruction and assessment. The U.S. Department of Education Office of Special Education and Rehabilitative Services notes that access is not just a special education concern, and that "all students benefit when the general education curriculum becomes more accessible" (*Federal Register,* 1999, p. 1470). During differentiated instruction, educators provide all students with access to the general education curriculum by varying "the learning activities, content demands, modes of assessment, and the classroom environment to meet the needs and support the growth of each child" (Thousand, Villa, & Nevin, 2015, p. 11). Differentiation requires attention to the following four design points when planning instruction:

1. *Facts about the students.* Levels of readiness and interest, learning strengths and challenges, primary languages and forms of communication, hobbies and interests, cultural backgrounds
2. *Content and materials.* What is taught, what students are expected to learn, the items and technology they are to use, and how to make them available
3. *Products and assessments.* How students are to demonstrate learning and how educators are to assess their performance
4. *Processes of learning.* How to structure learning activities to facilitate student understanding

As Figure 7.1 shows, teachers can attend to these four design points using two approaches: retrofitting and Universal Design for Learning (UDL).

FIGURE 7.1

Two Approaches to Differentiated Instruction

Retrofitting	Universal Design for Learning
1. Plan for *content*—what to teach and how content is made available to students 2. Plan processes *of learning*—how to teach the content and facilitate learning 3. Plan for *products* and assessments—what students will produce to show they have learned 4. Consider *facts about the learners*—Are there students for whom what is planned is not a good match?	1. Gather *facts about the learners*—discover the characteristics and learning and social/emotional differences among the students or potential students in the class 2. Differentiate *content* demands—plan multilevel goals based on standards, multi-level and multisensory materials 3. Differentiate *product* demands—multiple means for students to express understanding of the curriculum including multilevel, authentic, and performance assessments 4. Differentiate *processes* of instruction—providing students multiple means of engaging with the curriculum
Reactive "after-the-fact" differentiation based upon discovery of mismatches between facts about one or more student learners and instructional content, process, and/or product demands	**Proactive** differentiation of instructional content, product, and process demands based on upfront assumptions of student diversity in multiple dimensions and investigation of students' varying characteristics

Retrofitting

We have worked with numerous teachers doing their best to "retrofit" or alter preexisting curriculum and instructional methods to help ensure that all students have access to the general education material. A retrofit approach allows educators to correct mismatches between the learning characteristics of particular students and the traditional way we have made the content, process, and products of education accessible to all students.

Because the term *retrofit* is derived from architecture, an architectural analogy may help clarify it. Think of a multistoried school building built in the 1950s or '60s. Was it built to allow access for all students? No, but it can be *made* accessible by performing a retrofit: adding elevators and ramps, widening doorways, changing bathroom configurations, and so on. Similarly, educators may need to perform a retrofit when students encounter barriers to accessing the general curriculum—for example, when a student who reads independently at the 3rd grade level is offered only texts written at a 6th grade level.

A retrofit approach, although it works, requires spending a lot of valuable time and creative energy to develop individualized accommodations and modifications for any number of students. Because retrofitting is always a *reactive* approach to adjusting learning structures not originally designed for a range of learning differences, there are those who would argue that it should not be included in a discussion of differentiation. However, we believe that retrofitting is something teachers *need* to know how to do. We acknowledge that readers may be at different stages of adopting differentiation. For beginners, retrofitting offers a starting point for remodeling or reconceptualizing the content, process, and product demands of lessons. Retrofitting is also useful when teachers realize that a lesson designed to be universally accessible is just not working for some students.

In order for educators to maximize retrofitting, they must compare information about particular students with classroom content, process, and product demands. In gathering facts about students, teachers must get to know their strenghts as well as their challenges. Focusing only on perceived deficits doesn't yield information on how to capitalize on students' strengths. The more challenges students appear to face, the more important it is to discover and use their strengths.

To illustrate the effectiveness of retrofitting, we send you back to Chapter 4 and the Creative Problem Solving (CPS) process applied to differentiate for Shamonique (pp. 87–90). Recall the 22 potential solutions students generated to enable Shamonique to participate and succeed with the general curriculum (see Figure 4.5). Once potential solutions are selected, combined, and enacted, their effectiveness with Shamonique as well as with the other students can be evaluated.

The CPS retrofit process and template used with Shamonique (see Figure 4.4) can be used with any student. Here we illustrate how it might be used with Anna, a 12th grade classmate of Alcides, Heydar, and Christina who is new to the school and biliterate in Spanish and English. Anna is succeeding in Ms. Chavez's social studies class but struggling in Mr. Woo's

12th grade language arts class. Mr. Woo, who is also new to Monarch High School, previously taught at exclusive preparatory high schools in the United States and South Korea, where he had little exposure to or experience with differentiated instruction. At the new teacher orientation, Mr. Woo was introduced to concepts and processes for differentiation, including the CPS retrofit process and template. He eagerly tried it out with Anna when he detected her struggles in his class.

First, Mr. Woo sat down with Anna to get to know her better and review her past records. Then, at the weekly departmental meeting, he engaged his language arts teacher colleagues in a five-minute brainstorming session to identify mismatches and generate potential solutions to them. The results of the brainstorming and the actions Mr. Woo took are shown in Figure 7.2. Notice that the three retrofit actions—adapting *content access* options by providing materials in Spanish as well as at a lower readability level in English, changing the *process* of instruction to include frequent quick and cooperative strategies (e.g., "think-pair-share") before questions and quizzes, and expanding *product* and *assessment* options by offering quizzes and texts in both English and Spanish and allowing audiorecorded responses for all students—seem to be succeeding in giving Anna curriculum access, peer support, a way of showing what she knows, and the opportunity to develop social relations with her new classmates. Those actions also provide Mr. Woo with kernels for expanded, upfront differentiation in future lessons. He is on his way to using the second and more powerful differentiation approach: Universal Design for Learning (UDL).

Universal Design for Learning

As a generic concept, *universal design* refers to the creation and design of products and environments such that they can be used without being modified. Curb cuts are an example of universal design: they are expensive to add after the fact but cost virtually nothing if designed in from the start, and they offer many benefits (easier wheelchair and stroller access to sidewalks, less joint stress for joggers).

FIGURE 7.2

CPS Retrofit for Anna and 12th Grade Language Arts Class Demands

Stage 1: Challenge Finding There is a likely mismatch between Anna's characteristics and 12th grade language arts class demands			
Stage 2: Fact Finding		**Stage 3: Problem Finding**	**Stage 4: Idea Finding**
Facts About Anna	Facts About 12th Grade Language Arts Content, Process, and Product Demands	*Mismatches Between Anna and Class Demands*	*Potential Solutions (Brainstorm 2–4 per Mismatch)*
Strengths/Interests/Preferences Biliterate in Spanish & English Enjoys telling stories and joking Empathetic Likes technology Loves listening to music on any electronic device (phone, iPad) **Multiple Intelligences** Musical Bodily-kinesthetic Interpersonal	*Content/Materials* Text and literature in English with 9th grade or higher readability Same expectations for all students *Process* Mostly lecture with few visuals or examples Students volunteer to read or answer questions Public correction of student errors Rarely uses classroom SmartBoard or document projector Students rarely use technology	**Text readability** level is too high, not allowing Anna to do homework, start homework in class, or pass quizzes and tests **Technology** is an interest, but is **rarely used** by the teacher and even more rarely by students	Provide lower readability level materials Provide materials in Spanish More in-class applications Reduce, modify, or eliminate homework Use visuals (e.g., PowerPoint, Prezi) Use technology (e.g., text-to-speech software; SmartBoard, Smartphone, electronic devices, educational software) Use a flipped class format with pod-casted lessons Have students blog Integrate music and movement into presentation and product options

continued

FIGURE 7.2 *(continued)*

CPS Retrofit for Anna and 12th Grade Language Arts Class Demands

Stage 1: Challenge Finding There is a likely mismatch between Anna's characteristics and 12th grade language arts class demands			
Stage 2: Fact Finding		**Stage 3: Problem Finding**	**Stage 4: Idea Finding**
Challenges/Goals New to the school No friends yet Literacy level in Spanish is close to grade level Literacy level in English is at least four years below grade level Auditory processing difficulty Does not volunteer or answer questions or otherwise participate in class Does not do homework Failing tests and most quizzes Easily frustrated; throws objects and curses in both English and Spanish		Most **instruction is auditory** (lecture) and Anna is a bodily-kinesthetic, interpersonal, and musical learner with auditory processing difficulties **Limited social interaction** available in class to develop relationships with peers; Anna does not participate, as **public correction** is embarrassing	Provide lecture guides, graphic organizers, and structured notes Have students create graphic organizers Show video version of text Use partner and cooperative group learning Use quick cooperative structures such as "think-pair-share" every 5–10 minutes to digest information before a question or quiz Assign in-class buddies as mentors/tutors
	Product/Assessment Begins homework in class Homework from text assigned 4 nights/week Weekly quizzes and monthly tests based on homework Grades are partly based upon volunteering and answering questions	**Products/assessments** limited to written quizzes and tests in English with class participation points	Administer tests orally or in Spanish Expand assessment methods Develop with students a menu of product/assessment options with assessment rubrics Use humor—Have Anna and classmates come up with stories to act out what they have learned

Facts About Anna	Facts About 12th Grade Language Arts Content, Process, and Product Demands	*Mismatches Between Anna and Class Demands*	*Potential Solutions (Brainstorm 2–4 per Mismatch)*
		Classroom materials, instruction, and assessment prompt **frustration,** as does English literacy level	Refer Anna for Tier 2 reading intervention Conduct a Functional Behavioral Assessment of frustration behaviors Develop a behavioral contract

Stage 5: Solution Finding (Select preferred solutions using preferred evaluation criteria.)

Evaluation Criteria: Will it benefit other students? Is it easy to implement? Does it hold the student(s) accountable for content?

Solutions:
1. Provide lower readability materials; reduce/modify homework, with materials of lower readability
2. Use quick cooperative structures such as "think-pair-share" every 5–10 minutes to process information before questioning and before quizzes
3. Offer quizzes in Spanish and English and allow audio recorded responses for any student

continued

FIGURE 7.2 *(continued)*

CPS Retrofit for Anna and 12th Grade Language Arts Class Demands

Stage 6: Acceptance Finding *Action Plan* (Who does what, when? Is the plan working?)			
Activities (List preparation and implementation steps in order)	***Success Measure and Date or Timeline***	***Responsible Person(s)***	***Outcomes***
Provide lower readability materials; reduce/modify homework, with materials of lower readability	Anna completes homework and passes quizzes (within 3 weeks)	Anna and classroom teacher	Anna passed the last 2 of 3 quizzes. It seems to be helping.
Use quick cooperative structures such as "think-pair-share" every 5–10 minutes to process information before questioning and before quizzes	Anna participates with partners and answers questions and/or volunteers information (within 3 weeks)	Anna, classmates, and classroom teacher	It worked!
Offer quizzes in Spanish and English and allow audio-recorded responses for any student	Anna chooses Spanish or English versions and whether to use a recorded response option and passes quizzes (within 3 weeks)	Anna and classroom teacher	Anna has chosen Spanish quiz versions for multiple choice questions and the recorded response option for essays. Anna passed the last 2 of 3 quizzes.

When applied to education, the concept is known as Universal Design for Learning (UDL). Differentiated materials, methods, and assessment alternatives are considered and created in advance with the full range of students' differences in mind. The school makes audio and other alternatives to reading materials available that are of high interest and multiple levels of difficulty. Teachers take advantage of natural peer supports and instructional technologies that reflect best educational practices. They routinely use partner learning, cooperative group learning, integrated thematic units and lessons, and hands-on learning experiences. They bring the community to the classroom and the classroom to the community by incorporating service learning and technology into lessons. They use authentic assessment methods such as curriculum-based assessment, artifact collections and portfolios, individual learning contracts, and demonstrations. Meyer, Rose, and colleagues at the Center for Applied Special Technology first identified the three main goals of UDL (Meyer, Rose, & Gordon, 2014): to provide students with multiple means of *representation*, multiple means of *engagement*, and multiple means of *expression* (National Center for Universal Design for Learning, n.d.).

As Figure 7.1 shows, initiating UDL requires educators to first gather facts about students and then consider the aforementioned access points of content, product, and process, which directly reflect the three main UDL goals. Specifically, *content* requires multiple representations of lesson material, *process* requires engaging students in multiple ways, and *product* requires allowing students multiple methods of expressing their learning. The remainder of this chapter shows how to shift from a reactive retrofit approach to a proactive UDL approach to curriculum access.

The Four UDL Design Points

Figure 7.3 shows the four primary design points of the UDL approach to differentiation.

FIGURE 7.3

Universal Design for Learning: Four Design Points and Considerations

Design Point #1: Gathering Facts about Student Learners	What are each student's social and academic abilities, strengths, learning preferences, interests, cultural background and language(s)? What form of communication (e.g., primary language, assistive technology, Braille) does each student use to access information?	
Design Point #2: Content Differentiation Considerations	**Design Point #3: Product Differentiation Considerations**	**Design Point #4: Process Differentiation Considerations**
What are state curriculum and career readiness standards? *What are curriculum recommendations from professional organizations?*	*What are the product options and how will they be assessed?*	*Instructional Formats* Integrated cross-curricular thematic Inquiry-based learning Web-based, online learning Hands-on, activity-based Self-directed study Group investigation Socratic dialogue Learning centers and stations Simulation and role play Service learning, community projects
In addition to academic goals, what are language, social, and affective goals?	*What multilevel assessments and criteria will be used?*	*Instructional Arrangements* Whole group Cooperative learning structures Partner learning and peer tutoring Teacher-directed small groups Independent work One-on-one tutorial (only as needed)

<table>
<tr>
<td>How will we differentiate level of knowledge or proficiency?</td>
<td rowspan="4">Which authentic products will be created and how will they be evaluated (e.g., rubrics)?
Curriculum-based assessment
Collage — Rap/song
Mnemonics — Blog
Choral responding — Play
Podcast — Collage
Photo Essay — Model
Simulation — Role play
Oral Presentation — Dance
Oral history — Probes
Commercial — Editorial
Written presentation
PowerPoint or Prezi
Teaching others
Interview analysis summary
Portfolio of work</td>
<td>Instructional Strategies
Research-based strategies
Taxonomies (Bloom's)
Multiple Intelligence theory
Integrating the arts</td>
</tr>
<tr>
<td>In what sequence will concepts/content be taught?</td>
<td>Social Climate and Physical Environment
Social norms
Teaching social skills
Room arrangement for collaboration
Use of spaces outside of classroom
Positive behavior supports</td>
</tr>
<tr>
<td>What multilevel, multisensory, and multicultural materials will best convey concepts and content?</td>
<td rowspan="2">Co-Teaching Approaches
Supportive
Parallel
Complementary
Team</td>
</tr>
<tr>
<td>How will technology (e.g., text-to-speech software) provide access?</td>
</tr>
</table>

Design Point 1: Facts about Students

For all educators, the process of differentiating curriculum and instruction begins by knowing their students (see the top of Figure 7.3). Developing positive profiles of students' abilities, strengths, and learning challenges is an essential first step, as they can reveal pertinent strategies for effective teaching.

One useful framework for finding all students' strengths is the widely used theory of Multiple Intelligences (MI), originally proposed in the early 1980s by Howard Gardner (2011). After much research, Gardner concluded that existing ideas about intelligence were too narrow, and that all learners possess a mix of intelligence types that can be cultivated to emerge in unique configurations. The MI theory proposes the following eight types of intelligence:

1. *Verbal/linguistic.* Word-oriented; sensitive to the sound, structure, meaning, and function of words; may show affinity to storytelling, writing, reading, and verbal play (e.g., jokes, puns, riddles)

2. *Logical/mathematical.* Concept-oriented; able to perceive logical or numerical patterns; has a knack for discovering and testing hypotheses
3. *Visual/spatial.* Image- and picture-oriented; able to perceive the world visually and to transform those perceptions; may demonstrate artistic, designer, or inventive qualities
4. *Musical/rhythmic.* Melody- and rhythm-oriented; can produce and appreciate rhythm, pitch, timbre, and multiple forms of musical expression; may be animated or calmed by music
5. *Bodily/kinesthetic.* Physically oriented; uses body movements for self-expression (acting, dancing, mime); uses touch to interpret the environment; can skillfully handle or produce objects requiring fine-motor abilities; may excel in athletics
6. *Interpersonal.* Socially oriented; has strong mediation and leadership skills; can teach others and discern their moods, temperaments, and motivations
7. *Intrapersonal.* Intuitively oriented; can access and interpret his or her own feelings; may be strong-willed and self-motivated; may prefer solitary activities
8. *Naturalist.* capable of classifying nature; has exceptional knowledge of and sensitivity to things that exist in the natural world; can discern patterns (Gardner, 2011)

The MI profiles of Alcides, Heydar, Christina and other students (see Figure 7.4) can be helpful to Ms. Chavez as she considers potential materials and instructional processes that can capitalize on her students' diverse strengths and intelligences, cultivate areas of weakness or intelligences that are less evident, and optimize student responsiveness.

FIGURE 7.4

Multiple Intelligences Characteristics of Alcides, Heydar, and Christina

Student	Areas of Intelligence	Description
Alcides	Verbal/linguistic	Expresses himself well verbally in public settings
	Logical/mathematical	Excels in mathematics, enjoys data analysis, readily applies technology
	Visual/spatial	Has an affinity for technology, Internet research
	Musical/rhythmic	Plays the trumpet well
	Bodily-kinesthetic	Enjoys and excels in sports, particularly soccer
	Interpersonal	Is well-liked by peers and was elected school board student representative
	Intrapersonal	Prefers to work alone
	Naturalist	Is passionate about environmental issues
Heydar	Verbal/linguistic	Fluent and articulate in Arabic; learning English
	Logical/mathematical	Interested in anything mechanical, can solve technological problems by taking things apart
	Interpersonal	Readily approaches others in a cooperative and friendly manner
	Visual/spatial	Draws pictures to communicate; shows ability in photography and graphic arts
Christina	Verbal/linguistic	Gains information from conversations, partner and cooperative group learning structures; possesses a sense of humor
	Visual/spatial	Gains information readily from visual presentations and representation, including pictures, drawings, graphic organizers
	Interpersonal	Expresses empathy in relationships; is social with others and enthusiastic about friendship development and life, in general

Design Point 2: Content

Content has multiple dimensions, including what is to be taught; the sequence in which it will be taught; the level of knowledge or proficiency students are to demonstrate; and the necessary multilevel, multisensory, and multicultural materials, including technology, for allowing all students a point of entry to learning (see the left column of Figure 7.3 for content considerations).

Content is not formulated, selected, or delivered in a vacuum; it is hugely influenced by public policy, recommendations from professional education organizations, and state academic standards. High standards have become a national rallying cry. The Elementary and Secondary Education Act of 1965 (most recently reauthorized in 2015 as the Every Student Succeeds Act) requirements for accountability for all students' learning and the 2004 IDEIA reauthorization mandate for curriculum access ensure that students with disabilities are included in the call for high standards.

Every state has adopted curriculum standards, frameworks, and assessment systems that drive the content decisions that teachers must make each day. Although standards provide broad parameters for the content of a lesson or unit, educators must consider students' academic and social needs if they are to create meaningful learning experiences from the broad guidelines. Facts about students' MI profiles, past learning experiences, prior knowledge, and current interests and abilities are invaluable in designing students' multilevel goals and objectives.

We want all students to acquire and use knowledge meaningfully. However, the scope and degree of their mastery will vary. Any lesson, unit, or classroom featuring a diversity of abilities will likely feature multilevel goals and a focus on social and language learning as well as academic learning. Though all students engage in the same curricular content, it is presented with more or less complexity for each and may require an increased or decreased rate of completion or pacing as well as differentiated expectations from student to student. Some students may also have more personally meaningful or functional applications of content than others (Bambara, Koger, Burns, & Singley, 2016). For example, in a math class where students are working on story problems, a student who is learning English is given story problems that contain the English vocabulary she has been learning. In the same class, pairs of students are collaborating to solve long division problems. In one pairing, a student who struggles with multiple-digit subtraction focuses on the subtraction sub-problems while his partner focuses on the division aspects of the problems. In another pairing, one student uses manipulatives to assist in her understanding of division, while her partner, who has complex disabilities and more extensive support needs, focuses on visual tracking and object discrimination IEP goals by responding to cues and prompts from his partner to look at and follow the movement of the various colored manipulatives.

Design Point 3: Product

The third design point in the UDL process requires educators to determine what students will produce to demonstrate their learning (see the middle column of Figure 7.3 for product considerations). Although it may seem counterintuitive to decide on the products and assessments of a lesson *before* designing the lesson itself, this process, known as *backward design*, is a best practice for ensuring that lesson elements are designed with performance expectations and assessments in mind (Wiggins & McTighe, 2005; 2011).

For students to create products that accurately reflect their learning, educators must develop multiple ways for them to do so (for examples, see the middle column of Figure 7.3). Falvey and colleagues point out that educators often struggle with the question "How smart is this student?" when the real question to ask, according to Gardner, is "How *is* the student smart?" We want to presume that all students are smart, just in different ways (Falvey, Blair, Dingle, & Franklin, 2000, p. 194).

Design Point 4: Process

Process concerns instructional strategies that afford students multiple means of engaging with the curriculum. Since the original promulgation of IDEA in 1975, a tremendous amount of research has yielded effective instructional processes for helping students with and without disabilities to access curriculum, including "learning-to-learn" strategies, using constructivist principles to have students discover and construct their own knowledge, positive approaches to supporting challenging behavior (described in Chapter 5), collaborative planning and co-teaching among general and special educators (described in Chapters 4 and 6), engaging students as co-teachers, and connecting school and community through service learning and community-based projects. As noted in the right column of Figure 7.3, when planning lessons and units, the differentiating process requires educators to make decisions about instructional formats; instructional arrangements; instructional strategies; the social climate and physical environment of the classroom; and the use of co-teaching approaches.

Instructional format. The organizational design of a learning experience dictates how information is imparted to students and how they will interact with it. Teachers may choose from many instructional formats, such as those noted in Figure 7.3, that go beyond traditional lectures and direct instruction. Because these formats allow for multisensory experiences and are more active and interactive, they offer students greater opportunities for participation.

Instructional arrangements. Student configurations dictate whether students will work alone, as part of a large group, or with a small number of classmates. The key is to vary instructional arrangements across a day and week to achieve a calculated balance of large-group or whole-class instruction; teacher-directed small-group instruction; cooperative learning groups; partner learning and peer tutoring; and independent work. One-on-one instruction is rarely necessary and should be avoided as much as possible. However, when it is deemed warranted, the natural support of classmates and the teacher or co-teachers is preferable. Additional personnel such as paraeducators should be included only if educators have a clear goal to phase the arrangement out over time, as it can be isolating for students.

Instructional strategies. These are "teaching/learning techniques that help to make learners become well understood, help to make a skill become automatic, or help to readily transfer from one person to another a piece of knowledge" (Thousand, Villa, & Nevin, 2015, p. 133). Instructional strategies include educators' explicit and implicit directions, cues, prompts, and corrective feedback; questions that engage students in higher-order thinking; checks for understanding; behavior management techniques; and methods of providing physical assistance. Why not consider integrating the visual and performing arts as a strategy for differentiating instruction by tapping into students' multiple intelligences (e.g., visual/spatial, musical/rhythmic, bodily/ kinesthetic)?

Marzano, Pickering, and Pollock (2001) have identified nine categories of instructional strategies (e.g., cooperative group learning, setting objectives, and providing feedback) that research has shown to have strong effects on student achievement. We encourage you to learn more about how to use each of these strategies (see, for example, Dean, Hubbell, Pittner, & Stone, 2011; Marzano, Norford, Paynter, Pickering, & Gaddy, 2001) and think about how to effectively incorporate them into your teaching processes. We also encourage you to review instructional strategies that have met the research-evidence test required by the U.S. Office of Education by visiting the website of the Institute of Education Sciences: What Works Clearinghouse (http://ies.ed.gov/ncee/wwc/default.aspx).

Social climate and physical environment. The social climate and physical environment include such considerations as the room arrangement, accessibility of materials, regulation of visual and auditory distractions, and strategic seating of individual students. Establishing social norms governing movement, property, and interpersonal relations sets the overall climate, activity level, and interaction patterns during a lesson and throughout the day. Deliberately teaching social skills (e.g., waiting one's turn and raising hands to answer a question) are also integral to creating optimal environmental conditions.

Teachers can adjust the social climate and classroom norms to make learning more effective for students who need to be active (e.g., bodily/kinesthetic learners) and interactive (e.g., verbal/linguistic learners). Such shifts also require teachers to directly teach and expect students to use interpersonal, self-regulatory, and problem-solving social skills and strategies (such as the SODAS IF strategy discussed in Chapter 4). In other words, the teaching and practicing responsible behavior become priority curriculum domains, as they should be (Villa, Thousand, & Nevin, 2010).

Co-teaching approaches. The four main co-teaching approaches for process differentiation—supportive, parallel, complementary, and team—are discussed in detail in Chapter 6. Students as well as adults can take on co-teaching roles through cooperative groups, partner teaching, reciprocal teaching, and peer tutoring. (See Villa, Thousand, & Nevin [2010] for in-depth descriptions of the multiple ways students can differentiate instruction as co-teachers.)

When students actively communicate their understanding of content, their retention and achievement levels tend to increase. Reciprocal teaching, in which students alternate coaching one another, has been found to significantly raise and maintain the reading comprehension of struggling readers (Paliscar & Brown, 1984). Similarly, decades of research show that cooperative group learning helps students not only do better academically, but also to gain social competence, social acceptance, and an overall enjoyment of the subject matter when they work as reciprocal, positively interdependent co-teachers (Johnson & Johnson, 1989). Engaging students as co-teachers elicits student voice and helps them to acquire a greater awareness of their strengths and contributions.

Pause and Reflect on Technological and Student-Specific Supports

At each of the four design points, it is important for teachers, especially those new to the UDL process, to *pause and reflect* on whether or not specific students or the whole class could benefit from additional technological supports and individualization (e.g., connecting content to students' culture or home life). Fortunately, educational technology and web-based resources now are readily and easily available at little or no cost to help educators personalize learning. For example, the Kansas State Department of Education has collaborated with the Kansas Technical Assistance Support Network to create the KSDE TASN Co-Teaching Differentiated Instruction Resource

Pages (found at **https://sites.google.com/site/ksdetasndi2/home**), a database of links to a host of online resources for getting to know learners better and differentiating at the content, product, and processes design points. Thousand, Villa, and Nevin (2015) also describe web-based tools that can be integrated into almost any lesson to help differentiate instruction.

An Example of UDL in Action

Ms. Chavez, introduced earlier in this chapter, teaches an integrated English and social studies course in a 90-minute extended block at Monarch High School. As one of the first steps to introducing her new unit of study, she told her students that they would be studying Cold War tensions between the United States and communist countries, with a focus on the Vietnam War. She then shared the following standards to be addressed during the unit:

- Analyze ideological differences and other factors that contributed to the Cold War and to U.S. involvement in conflicts intended to contain communism (e.g., Vietnam War).
- List the effects of foreign policy on domestic policies and vice versa (e.g., protests against the Vietnam War).
- Examine constitutional issues involving war powers as they related to U.S. military intervention in Vietnam.
- Compare and contrast public support of the U.S. government and military during the Vietnam War with that of other conflicts.
- Analyze the media's role in bringing information to the public and shaping public attitudes toward the Vietnam War. (See the 2014 New Jersey Core Curriculum Content Standards for Social Studies at http://www.state.nj.us/education/cccs/2014/ss/.)

To solicit students' prior knowledge and determine the direction of the unit, Ms. Chavez engaged her class in a variation of a Know, Want to Know, and Learned (KWL) strategy by asking them to complete a chart showing what they want to know about the Vietnam War, how they want to learn about the war, and how they want to show her what they've learned about the war. In reviewing the students' responses, Ms. Chavez noted some weaknesses in her students' knowledge base. She asked them to continue thinking about the three questions for homework, and also asked them to ask their grandparents and neighbors about the war.

The following day, Ms. Chavez and the students compiled the information about the *content* they wanted to learn, the *processes* that they would use to learn it, and the types of *products* that they could produce to demonstrate what they'd learned. The results are shown in Figure 7.5.

Ms. Chavez's modified KWL activity resulted in a menu from which each student could choose three methods to convey his or her knowledge about the Vietnam War at the unit's end (see Figure 7.6). Ms. Chavez met with students individually to review the curriculum standards and the list of what students wanted to learn about the war to select the focus of each student's work. Students were to engage in at least one activity with a partner or group and complete at least one activity alone.

Remember Ms. Chavez's students Alcides, Heydar, and Christina? Alcides used his musical/rhythmic, mathematical/logical, and naturalistic intelligences as vehicles to access the curriculum, participate in learning activities, and demonstrate his knowledge. Two of his learning goals were taking perspective and analyzing data, so his product was a written report exploring the immediate and long-term costs of the Vietnam War. He wrote about the amount of money expended by the U.S. and Vietnamese governments, the types and amounts of armaments used, lives lost, the number of people who were left homeless, the effects of the war on Vietnam's neighbors, and the long-term effects of the war on people's health and the environment.

To strengthen Alcides's interpersonal skills, other students provided him with data that they collected during their research, and he created and presented tables and graphs to summarize them. In a second project, Alcides used music-editing software to digitize bits from songs and political speeches of the era in an original piece of music that synthesized various perspectives on the war.

Heydar's visual/spatial and interpersonal strengths as well as his life experiences shaped his selection of learning activities. Given his need to

FIGURE 7.5

Modified KWL Strategy to Determine Focus of the Unit

<table>
<tr><th colspan="2">Content (What do you want to know about the Vietnam War?)</th></tr>
<tr><td>

Student-Generated
Why did we fight the war?
Why didn't we win the war?
How many people died?
What kinds of weapons were used?
What was the impact of the war on their society and ours?
What role did music play, if any?
Why were so many people opposed to the war?
What happened to the people who refused to fight in the war?
How did the war end?
Which countries were our allies and which were our enemies?
What is communism? Why was it considered bad?
What kind of government does Vietnam have now?
What was it like to fight there?
What is Agent Orange?
Has Vietnam fought in other wars? Did Vietnam win them?

Source Materials to Learn this Information
History texts
First-person narratives (written and person-to-person contacts)
Content from the Internet, newspapers, books, political cartoons
News programs, documentaries, and movies from that time and about that time
(e.g., *Deer Hunter, Good Morning Vietnam*)

</td><td>

Teacher Additions
Was the war limited to Vietnam?
How were people selected to fight in the war?
What was the cost of the war (e.g., fiscal, human loss, effect on other social initiatives in the U.S.)?
What role did the media play? Should the media have done anything differently?
In what ways did we dehumanize the Vietnamese?
What effect, if any, did the Vietnam War have on public acceptance of U.S. military involvement in subsequent war and incursions?
How did the war affect U.S. and Vietnamese society?
How are U.S.-Vietnam governmental relations today? Are there any unresolved issues?
How were veterans treated then compared to now?
How does Vietnam compare to current and 20th Century wars?
What dimensions of comparison are relevant?

Teacher Additions to Source Materials
Book (e.g., *The Pentagon Papers*)
Biography (e.g., John McCain)

</td></tr>
</table>

continued

FIGURE 7.5

Modified KWL Strategy to Determine Focus of the Unit

Process (How do you want to learn about the Vietnam War?)
Work alone, in pairs, or in cooperative groups. Work in learning stations with topics of interest to share resources and discuss ideas. Read texts individually and/or discuss in group literature circles. Interview people who fought in the war, people who favored the war, and people who were opposed to the war. Conduct Internet and library research to review books and newspaper stories from the time. Analyze and critique media from that era (e.g., political cartoons). Engage in simulations and role-plays to understand perspectives of others.
Products (How do you want to show me what you have learned about the war?)
Give an oral report (e.g., presentation, debate). Submit a written report (e.g., essay report, PowerPoint or Prezi presentation). Create a visual presentation (e.g., drawings, posters, cartoon strips). Create graphic and mathematical (e.g., timeline) summaries that compare and contrast the United States and Vietnam across several dimensions (e.g., economic structure, resources, population diversity, geography, military resources, allies, religions, imports and exports, political system). Articulate a personal position in a persuasive way about whether the war should have been fought, whether or not nuclear weapons should have been used to end the war, and so on.

practice English, his work alone was minimized. Ms. Chavez arranged for him to accompany other students on interviews and take pictures of the interviewees and their artifacts from the war, such as medals and letters. Some of the men in the homeless shelter where Heydar was staying noticed him and his uncle working on the project and told them that they were veterans. With the aid of his uncle, who spoke English, Heydar interviewed them.

For Heydar's learning product, one of the paraeducators at the school who speaks Arabic interpreted for him so that he could verbally present his interviews. Heydar also drew pictures to illustrate the effects of the Vietnam War and contrasted them with his own experiences in Libya.

Christina's selection of relevant content, processes, and products was influenced by her interpersonal, musical/rhythmic, and verbal/linguistic strengths as well as by her empathetic nature. With the teacher's assistance,

FIGURE 7.6

Menu of Methods and Product Choices for Vietnam War Unit

Verbal/Linguistic	**Logical/Mathematical**	**Visual/Spatial**
Oral presentation Debate Interview PowerPoint or Prezi presentation Other:	Charts Graphs Timeline such as timeline of critical events Statistical analysis Extrapolation of data Other:	Photojournalism Posters Murals Graphic art pieces (e.g., cartoons, drawings) or displays Other:
Musical/Rhythmic Poetry Rap Analysis of music of the times Original piece of music Other:	**Topic:** **Vietnam War**	**Bodily/Kinesthetic** Dramatic presentation of a scene, concept, or critical issue Interpretive dance Use mime or gestures Other:
Intrapersonal Fictional diary entries written from the perspective of a U.S. or Vietnamese soldier, draft dodger, conscientious objector, parent who has one child fighting in the war and one child protesting the war Other:	**Interpersonal** Interviews with people holding different perspectives about the war Other:	**Naturalist** Examine the impact of the war on the environment and people (e.g., Agent Orange, land mines) Other:

she developed interview questions for a Vietnam War veteran, a former war protestor, and a Vietnamese émigré to the United States. She traveled by bus with a peer to conduct the first two interviews and then on her own to conduct the third. With the help of word-prediction software and peer editing, she wrote a paragraph summarizing each of the three interviews.

In an oral presentation, she explained to her classmates the similarities and differences among the interviewees' positions, and excerpts from one of her interviews appeared on the school's morning newscast. Another of Christina's projects involved listening to songs from the Vietnam War era and identifying whether they expressed pro- or antiwar sentiments.

Christina identified specific words and phrases within the songs to justify her conclusions.

While learning about the Vietnam War, Christina addressed three of her six priority IEP goals: staying engaged in class activities and discussions by making comments or asking questions; writing short paragraphs with peer and technology support; and traveling independently in the community.

Using the UDL process outlined in this chapter, Ms. Chavez was able to design instruction that effectively promoted active and meaningful participation for the full range of students in her class, including Alcides, Heydar, and Christina.

Final Thoughts

Engaging in curricular and instructional differentiation is an act of *change.* As Leo Buscaglia said, "Change. It has the power to uplift, to heal, to stimulate, surprise, open new doors, bring fresh experience and create excitement in life. Certainly it is worth the risk" (Buscaglia, n.d.).

The retrofit and UDL decision-making processes described in this chapter are intended not only to demystify the work of differentiation, but also to serve as collaborative tools for facilitating changes in thought and practice to grant curriculum access to all students. We recognize that changing or refining our practices may feel risky and, at times, uncomfortable. However, we also recognize that it is in this state of temporary imbalance that the most creative solutions are generated.

References

Bambara, L. M., Koger, F., Burns, R. & Singley, D. (2016). Building skills for home and community. In F. Brown, J. McDonnell, & M. E. Snell (Eds.). *Education students with severe disabilities* (8th ed., pp. 438–473). Boston: Pearson.

Buscaglia, L. (n.d.). AZQuotes.com. Retrieved from www.azquotes.com/quote/565197.

Carr, E. G., & Ogle, D. (1987). KWL plus: a strategy for comprehension and summarization. *Journal of Reading, 21*(8), 684–689.

Center for Applied Special Technology (CAST). (2008). *Universal design for learning guidelines: Version 1.0.* Wakefield, MA: Author. Retrieved from http://www.udlcenter.org/sites/udlcenter.org/files/guidelines.pdf.

Dean, C. B., Hubbell, E. R., Pitler, H., & Stone B. (2011). *Classroom instruction that works: Research-based strategies for increasing student achievement* (2nd ed.) Alexandria, VA: ASCD.

Falvey, M., Blair, M., Dingle, M. P., & Franklin, N. (2000). Creating a community of learners with varied needs. In R. A. Villa & J. S. Thousand (Eds.), *Restructuring for caring and effective education: An administrative guide to creating heterogeneous schools* (2nd ed., pp. 186–207). Baltimore: Paul H. Brookes.

Federal Register. (1999, March 12). *Rules and regulations, 64*(48). Washington, DC: U.S. Government Printing Office.

Gardner, H. (2011). *Frames of mind: The theory of multiple intelligences* (3rd ed.). New York: Basic Books.

Individual with Disabilities Education Improvement Act of 2014, PL 108-446, 20 U.S.C. §§1400 et seq.

Johnson, D. W., & Johnson, R. T. (1989). *Cooperation and competition: Theory and research.* Edina, MN: Interaction Book Company.

Marzano, R. J., Norford, J. S., Paynter, D. E., Pickering, D. J., & Gaddy, B. B. (2001). *A handbook for classroom instruction that works.* Alexandria, VA: ASCD.

Marzano, R., Pickering, D., & Pollock, J. (2001). *Classroom instruction that works: Research-based strategies for increasing student achievement.* Alexandria, VA: ASCD.

Meyer, A., Rose, D. H., & Gordon, D. (2014). *Universal design for learning: Theory and practice.* Wakefield, MA: CAST Professional Publishing.

National Center on Universal Design for Learning. (n.d.). *UDL guidelines: Version 2.0.* Retrieved from http://www.udlcenter.org/aboutudl/udlguidelines.

Paliscar, A. S., & Brown, A. (1984). Reciprocal teaching of comprehension: Fostering and monitoring activities. *Cognition and Instruction, 1*(2), 117–175.

Thousand, J., Villa, R., & Nevin, A. (2015). *Differentiating instruction: Planning for universal design and teaching for college and career readiness* (2nd ed.). Thousand Oaks, CA: Corwin.

Udvari-Solner, A., Villa, R. A., & Thousand, J. S. (2005). Access to the general education curriculum for all: The universal design process. In R. A, Villa & J. S. Thousand (Eds.), *Creating an inclusive school* (2nd ed., pp. 134–155). Alexandria, VA: ASCD.

Villa, R. A., & Thousand, J. S. (2005). *Creating an inclusive school* (2nd ed.). Alexandria, VA: ASCD.

Villa, R. A., Thousand, J. S., & Nevin, A. (2010). *Collaborating with students in instruction and decision making: The untapped resource.* Thousand Oaks, CA: Corwin.

Villa, R. A., & Thousand, J. S. (2011). *RTI: Co-teaching and differentiated instruction.* Port Chester, NY: National Professional Resources.

Wiggins, G., & McTighe, J. (2005). *Understanding by design* (2nd ed., expanded). Alexandria, VA: ASCD.

Wiggins, G., & McTighe, J. (2011). *Understanding by design for high-quality units.* Alexandria, VA: ASCD.

CHAPTER 8

Access and Success for All: What Can One Person Do?

Jacqueline S. Thousand and Richard A. Villa

If you have read Chapters 3 through 7 in sequence, you have taken in a tremendous amount of information about how to structure inclusive schools from the bottom up using the Schoolhouse Model framework. You now know a great deal about critical actions for administrators, collaborative creative problem solving, the Multitiered System of Supports, co-teaching structures, and both the retrofit and Universal Design for Learning processes for differentiating instruction. While all of these structures and actions can allow every student access to, and success in, the general education curriculum, contemplating where and how to start implementing can be overwhelming.

What if you're one of only a committed few in your community serious about fostering more inclusive schooling? What if you lack systems-level support for making inclusion a priority? What can one person do to lead the change? To begin to answer these questions, consider these words from Robert Kennedy's 1966 address to the young people of South Africa on their Day of Affirmation:

> Some believe there is nothing one man or one woman can do against the enormous array of the world's ills, against ignorance, injustice, misery, or suffering. Yet many of the world's greatest movements, of thought and action, have flowed from the work of a single person. A young monk began the Protestant Reformation, a young general extended an empire from Macedonia to the borders of the earth, and a young woman

reclaimed the territory of France. It was the 32-year-old Thomas Jefferson who proclaimed that all humans are created equal.

These people moved the world, and so can we all. Few will have the greatness to bend history itself, but each of us can work to change a small portion of events, and in the total of all of those acts will be written the history of this generation.

It is from the numberless diverse acts of courage and belief that human history is shaped. Each time a person stands up for an ideal, or acts to improve the lot of others, or strikes out against injustice, they send forth a tiny ripple of hope, and crossing each other from a million different centers of energy and daring, those ripples build a current that can sweep down the mightiest walls of oppression and resistance.

What You Can Do

So, what can one person do? First, believe that you can make a difference, even though it may be small and even if the system is not yet behind you.

Next, take action in areas where you have control, such as your own classroom. For example, try co-teaching with a colleague, intervention specialist, or paraeducator, or try using the retrofit approach to solving a student-instructional mismatch. Learn more about inclusive education best practices, UDL, co-teaching, and student empowerment strategies by reading Villa and Thousand (2016), Thousand, Villa, and Nevin (2015), and Villa, Thousand, and Nevin (2010). Try out a couple of upfront differentiation strategies. Build in peer-mediated learning processes such as cooperative learning, reciprocal teaching, and partner learning structures throughout the day and week.

Take action with people in your immediate sphere of influence and trusted colleagues. Experiment with some of the creative problem-solving processes offered in Chapter 4 with one or more teams at your school. Invite a general or special educator you know to co-teach with you, even if only for 30 to 40 minutes a week, and help you try out some of the strategies discussed in Chapter 7. Recommend this book to other teachers, parents, and administrators. Initiate a book study group with a group of like-minded educators and agree to a doable plan for activating or enhancing any dimension of the Schoolhouse Model at your school.

Be even more proactive and expansive in your leadership. Recruit a group of colleagues, including administrators, to attend a professional development seminar on UDL, positive behavior support strategies, or co-teaching. Then, you can put your heads together to craft an action plan for priority partnerships, structures, or strategies to foment schoolwide change. Or, invite your administrative team to pull together a group of teachers, parents, and students to examine the schoolwide discipline and academic support system to ensure that it aligns with best practices in MTSS or SWPBS, as discussed in Chapter 5. Use a tool such as *The Inclusive Education Checklist: A Self-Assessment of Quality Inclusive Education Practices* (Villa & Thousand, 2016) to assess your school's progress implementing the multiple dimensions of inclusion.

Act in any way you can think of to increase the number of people and the depth of their conviction to promote inclusion. Some advice:

- *Be the change you wish to see.* Model the inclusion of children and adults with diverse interests and abilities in both your professional and personal life.
- *Seeing is believing.* Locate or create a successful example of inclusive education in action and publicize it. Have people visit and talk with those involved in the effort.
- *There is strength in numbers.* Create support groups of families and others like yourself to strategize how to get broader support. Build coalitions among disability rights groups, civil rights groups, parent groups, and other groups inside and outside of your school. Educate others as to the ethical, legal, moral, research-based rationales for inclusive education. Share the information from this book with them.
- *Get into positions of power.* Run for the school board, become an officer of the teacher's union, or volunteer for local, regional, and statewide committees or taskforces that influence school policy.
- *Persevere and be compassionate.* Remember that changing people's minds and beliefs causes emotional turmoil and, therefore, takes time.

Final Thoughts

In closing, we return to the observation we made in the Letter to the Reader at the beginning of the book. Leadership is any action that promotes the accomplishment of tasks or builds interpersonal relations that can be harnessed to do so. In this case, the task at hand is creating inclusive educational opportunities. Taking action *is* leading an inclusive school.

References

Thousand, J. S., Villa, R. A., & Nevin, A. I. (2015). *Differentiating instruction: Planning for universal design and teaching for college and career readiness* (2nd ed.). Thousand Oaks, CA: Corwin.

Villa, R. A., Thousand, J. S., & Nevin, A. I. (2010). *Collaborating with students in instruction and decision making: The untapped resource.* Thousand Oaks, CA: Corwin.

Villa, R. A., Thousand, J. S., & Nevin, A. I. (2013). *A guide to co-teaching: New lessons and strategies to facilitate student learning* (3rd ed.). Thousand Oaks, CA: Corwin.

Villa, R. A., & Thousand, J. S. (2016). *The inclusive education checklist: A self-assessment of best practices.* Katonah, FL: National Professional Resources.

VOICE OF INCLUSION

The Principal's Role in Creating and Sustaining Inclusive Education

Yazmin Pineda Zapata

In this Voice of Inclusion, I offer the perspectives of 14 principals of elementary, middle, and high schools that have been identified as among the most inclusive in the United States.[1] For my dissertation, I conducted a study to identify principal leadership knowledge, skills, and behaviors associated with leading and sustaining inclusion efforts in schools. Here, I have organized the principals' responses according to the five variables of complex change discussed in Chapter 3: vision, skills, incentives, resources, and action planning. (I have used pseudonyms to maintain the respondents' anonymity.)

Vision

The core values in the schools studied emerged from principals who "were clear about their schools' fundamental mission" and for whom "inclusion was a non-negotiable grounded in civil rights" (Hehir & Katzmann, 2012, p. 33). When asked to define inclusion, the principals repeatedly referred to principles of social justice and to a broad spectrum of students beyond those with disabilities. Principal Brentwood said:

[1] The schools identified by one or more of the following organizations: School Wide Integrated Framework for Transformation, Maryland Coalition for Inclusive Education, ARC of Texas Inclusion Works organization, National Association for Persons with Severe Handicaps, California State University San Marcos Summer Leadership Institute organizers, and PEAK Parent Center in Colorado Springs, Colorado.

> All means all. . . . We don't discriminate based on the student's disability. . . . We go to great lengths to make sure [students'] needs are met in the classroom and outside of the classroom. . . . It's really a belief. . . . The best teachers are teachers that can teach all kids, not just kids who behave well or perform well academically. . . . The real teachers are the ones who teach all kids and they are passionate about that.

Similarly, principal Oakland noted that he is responsible for "aligning the virtues of inclusion and how that can be construed as an extension of and appreciation for diversity and [help] students and staff become sensitive to the needs of [every child]." Principals Kline and Rose also saw inclusion as part of a broader vision affording *all* kids with the same rich opportunity to learn.

Building Consensus for the Vision

Scruggs and Mastropieri (1996) and Waldron, McLeskey, and Redd (2011) note that principals must not only develop their own commitment to the core values of inclusive education, but also inspire their school community to build a consensus for an inclusionary vision. Change is most successful when led by principals who "understand the developmental change process and are able to nurture and challenge, while maintaining connections with their faculty and community members" (Salisbury & McGregor, 2005, p. 8).

The principals in this study had to garner buy-in from various stakeholders. They understood that they could not make their vision of inclusion and social justice a reality without teacher commitment, and they understood that gaining that commitment required them first to develop trusting relationships and then to continually communicate the vision until it became ingrained in the school culture. For example, Principal Jackson highlighted the importance of communicating the vision to such staff as food service workers, custodians, and bus drivers until it "was second nature." He appreciated these members of the school community as "an important part of the building" who added "a lot" to the change process.

The bottom line for these principals was achieving a culture where *all* staff, instructional and noninstructional, understood that their goal was to help all students be successful—a culture where, as Principal Rose put it,

> all students [could] be successful in whatever measure. . . . It's not always a certain score on a state assessment. . . . It may be success in developing social skills . . . learning to control their behavior . . . getting good movement of their arms. . . . [E]veryone in the school, teachers, paraprofessionals, administration, custodians, lunchroom [personnel], every person that work[ed] in the school work[ed] towards making all children successful.

Skills

Principals in this study varied in their experience, training, and skills relative to students with disabilities prior to taking on the task of establishing inclusion in their schools. A majority had no training in special education, a few had extensive experience working with students identified as having disabilities, and the rest fell somewhere in between. Regardless of this variability, the principals all tended to agree that a background in special education was *not* necessary to *believe* that all students could thrive in an inclusive environment with appropriate supports and services.

Many of the principals, particularly those without a background in special education, were driven by their passion for inclusion to seek out knowledge independently, and to develop their own skills for leading organizational change. In addition, they actively participated in professional development with their teachers and staff to demonstrate that they were truly invested in and ready to collaborate on developing the best possible learning environment for all students.

Building Staff Capacity

The leaders interviewed did whatever it took to build the skills of their school staffs, using diverse resources such as university courses, professional development trainings, DVDs, books, and consistent and repeated classroom observations paired with feedback, modeling, and coaching.

Co-Teaching and Collaborative Planning

The principals highlighted co-teaching and collaborative planning as essential for creating dynamic inclusive classrooms. Through structured collaborative planning time, teachers learned to effectively communicate, share responsibility for students, and positively influence one another's teaching.

Professional Development for Everyone

Not surprisingly, ongoing professional development emerged as crucial to the transformation of the 14 schools studied. And it wasn't limited to faculty: custodians, lunch personnel, playground supervisors, bus drivers, parents, and students were all involved in training. Further, as Principal Jackson notes, professional development "wasn't just one of those 'fly in on the opening day of inservice, give the keynote, and then see you next year'" kind, but rather "pretty focused and pretty frequent."

Principals in this study were asked to identify the professional development areas that supported them the most in making inclusive education work. Overwhelmingly, they selected the following as their top-10 areas:

- The "why" of inclusion—namely, the social justice philosophy and belief system
- The "what" of inclusion—what it looks like and the specifics of each person's role
- The "free and appropriate public education" and "least restrictive environment" requirements of the Individual with Disabilities Education Improvement Act
- The characteristics of various disabilities
- Positive, proactive behavior support and classroom management strategies
- Collaborative teaming, planning, and problem solving that includes student voice
- Differentiated instruction and lesson planning using principles of Universal Design for Learning
- Co-teaching among general educators and specialists

- Shared responsibility for crafting and executing accommodations and modifications
- Use of assistive technology and augmentative communication with students

Teacher Leadership

Principals should empower teachers to assume leadership roles, share and analyze student data, and engage in shared decision making to further the change agenda (Waldron & McLeskey, 2010). The principals interviewed identified leveraging the skills and talents of their staffs to build buy-in and trust as very important. They were deliberate about establishing and using teacher leadership groups not only to identify training needs, but also to lead professional development sessions. For example, at Blue Middle School, a core team of teachers received extra release time for inclusion planning after attending their state's Coalition for Inclusive Education's trainings, which they also used to develop and deliver inclusion workshops for their colleagues. Principal Brentwood used a similar approach to develop his teachers' capacity to effectively support students developing English proficiency. As he described it, his goal was to "develop leaders within the program [who] have had the professional development, become experts in the subject, and then can implement the PD, too."

Coaching and Specialized Instruction

At several schools, principals engaged teachers as peer coaches to model, observe, and provide feedback on curriculum, differentiation, and effective instruction. At some schools, paraprofessionals received supplemental instruction in skills to, in Principal Fairfield's words, "integrate elegantly into a classroom where they are not only a specific support for a student with disabilities but a resource across the classroom." All principals identified training for parents as key to supporting inclusion—particularly for those whose children had spent many years in a segregated special education environment. These parents needed to develop trust in the system of inclusion and understand how it would benefit their children better than segregation.

Incentives

Salisbury and McGregor (2005) note that, "while the benefits of inclusive schooling will ultimately be the incentive to continue the effort required to maintain these practices, people need support along the way to help them reach a point of comfort and success" (p. 9).

Emotional Support and Appreciation

Principals in the study highlighted the importance of attending to the social-emotional needs of their staff. Four of the principals held daily debriefing sessions with general and special educators and other support providers and specialists—not only to discuss how well instruction and supports were working for students and collaboratively make adjustments, but also to tend to the staff's emotional needs and celebrate the successes of the day. Several principals spoke of the importance of giving new teachers a mentor both to coach them academically and to listen to their frustrations and celebrate their triumphs.

Celebrating teachers' hard work takes many forms. Several principals arranged for teachers to attend conferences and to lead professional development training for their peers. Many of them acknowledged staff formally and informally through the use of thank-you cards, positive feedback, certificates, and newsletters.

Logistical Support

Principals noted the importance of attending to basic workload equity and logistical issues. They talked about balancing caseloads based upon student needs, rearranging schedules to allow special educators and other support staff to be in general education classrooms at the most effective times, and setting up transition meetings so the upcoming year's teachers could collaborate with existing teachers and with parents to learn of and plan for the critical needs of individual students.

Time and Opportunity to Collaborate

Raywid (1993) notes that "[t]he time necessary to examine, reflect on, amend, and redesign programs is not auxiliary to teaching responsibilities—nor is it released time from them. It is absolutely central to such responsibilities, and essential to making school succeed" (p. 34). Is not time the eternal and ubiquitous incentive? Certainly, the principals in the study identified time as an essential incentive and resource. They made sure that staff were given time to collaborate on analyzing student data, planning curriculum, and evaluating their own practices to better meet the needs of their diverse learners. Principal Brentwood nicely described the principal's responsibility to carve out collaboration time for staff:

> What makes a really successful and inclusive environment is collaboration among all of the team members. . . . It is an absolutely huge part of it and that it's built into their day. . . . You don't say, as an administrator, "Oh, go find time to plan." You're actually building it into their day and saying, "I'm going to give you time as an administrator to work together." . . . Inclusion definitely does not happen in an isolated environment. You can't have teachers who are just working in the room and not talking to anyone. It will not work.

The collaboration time that principals offered, although it ranged in frequency and duration, was regularly structured into each school's schedule. Principals also understood how valuable supplemental time is for teachers, so they were flexible about providing full- or half-day substitutes to allow for more planning if teachers requested it. The teachers at the 14 schools also used summers to plan the opening days of school with their new students in mind.

Principal Fairfield described her school's approach to collaboration as "rigorous" and involving "a short debriefing at the end of the day . . . so that teachers could actively see each other using the tools they learned in their professional development. . . . It was inspiring for teachers to . . . mind-share and [provide] collegial support." All of the staff working in a classroom—general and special educators, service personnel, paraeducators—met to "reflect on the day . . . provide a collaborative experience . . . and get feedback from one another on how to . . . adjust the support for the following day." The benefits of these debriefings were threefold: they served to develop team members' *skills*, helped them to use *resources* more efficiently, and served as an *incentive* by meeting their emotional and technical needs and being built into the daily schedule.

Student Success

The principals in this study all noted that staff observance of student success not only validated the hard work and dedication they had put into transforming their classrooms, but was probably the single most influential incentive for staff. Many principals were certain that if the incentives they now provided somehow suddenly disappeared, the school community would not waiver in its commitment to inclusive education as long as students continued to succeed.

Resources

DuFour and Eaker (1998), Wenger (1998), and Wenger and Synder (2000) all emphasize the importance of providing resources to sustain learning communities, and the principals in the study also recognized their importance to achieving successful inclusion. Among the resources they cited as helpful were technology, instructional materials, collaboration opportunities, access to outside expertise, ongoing quality professional development, common planning time, equitably distributed special education caseloads, visits to conferences and model schools, and responsive student support systems.

Several principals acknowledged that securing funding for resources could pose a challenge, and all of them agreed that allocating funding to support inclusion should be a priority for which it was their responsibility to advocate. Principal Zach described the tension and responsibility:

> We have these great visions and we put them into motion and the staff supports them and backs them up, but then we sometimes lack the resources to carry those visions out. . . [My job is] identifying what those resources are and then making sure that we follow through with providing those so that the staff can see we're invested in seeing this thing through.

Action Planning

Vision, skills, incentives, and resources are actualized through action planning. Principals in the study were asked to identify the key components of their action plans and agreed on the following seven, each of which relates to at least one of the five variables of complex change:

1. Educating people on the philosophy—the "why"—of inclusion (vision)
2. Developing strong partnerships with parents (vision, resources)
3. Showing people what to do (e.g., redefining roles) and how to do it (skills)
4. Providing ongoing professional development, including workshops, consultations, and book studies (skills, resources)
5. Providing staff with time to debate, question, plan, and reflect (incentives, resources)
6. Establishing support systems for teachers and students (incentives, resources)
7. Showing all stakeholders that their input is valued (incentives, resources)

In describing his multi-year action plan, Principal Smith hit upon most of the above components and all four of the variables besides action planning. Here's his story of establishing and maintaining a collaborative and inclusive school:

> [W]e talked about beliefs and vision and mission, understanding the "why." . . . Because if people don't understand the "why" they're not going to be very inclined to try. We did the training. Gave them the foundational informational baseline. From there it became application. . . . They were working on real students. . . . They were trying. They were making errors, they were failing. But all along the way we were there encouraging and helping them grow and develop. At the same time, we continued ongoing training for two years. Currently, we still meet monthly with the special education teachers and we meet more often than that with the teams. We check in [when] the special ed. and the regular ed. people are planning together, just to see what they need. And again, still have those incentives when they're requested. "Can we get a day off?" Or, "Can we get a half

a day to really plan some things out with this co-teaching?" We still let them do that . . . administratively, we created the plan, but we're always collaborative, and we're always asking them, "What do you need? When do you need it? What else can we do to help? Can we videotape your room and show it to you?" I mean, we did that last week, so they could watch themselves, see what happens. We can learn so much more from videotaping and then studying each other and seeing what's good and what can be improved.

Conclusion

Vision without action is just a dream. Action without vision just passes the time. Vision and action combined can change the world.

The above quote is said to have begun as a Japanese proverb. It also has been attributed to the leadership guru Joel Barker and to Nelson Mandela. Regardless of its origins, the meaning is clear. Change is complex and requires attention to multiple variables. Vision or action are not enough.

The study of 14 principals from successful inclusive schools points to the importance of attending to each of the five key variables of complex change. Principals recognized the importance of developing a core *vision* of effective inclusion, but far more was needed. Quality strategic and ongoing professional development coupled with modeling and coaching (i.e., skills) matters. Clear structures and support systems for both students and staff (i.e., incentives and resources) matter. Outlining how to execute the vision (i.e., action planning) matters.

My hope in capturing and sharing the voice, vision, and actions of these 14 principals is to help clarify what dispositions, skills, and behaviors work best to create a clear, predictable, effective, and sustainable path to inclusive schooling.

References

DuFour, R., & Eaker, R. (1998). *Professional learning communities at work: Best practices for enhancing student achievement.* Bloomington, IN: Solution Tree.

Hehir, T. & Katzman, L. (2012). *Effective inclusive schools: Designing successful schoolwide programs.* San Francisco, CA: Jossey-Bass.

McLeskey, J., Waldron, N., & Redd, L. (2014). A case study of a highly effective inclusive elementary school. *The Journal of Special Education, 48*(1), 59–70.

Pineda, Y. (2015). A principal's role in creating and sustaining an inclusive environment (Unpublished doctoral dissertation). San Diego State University, San Diego.

Raywid, M.A. (1993). Finding time for collaboration. *Educational Leadership, 51*(1), 30–34.

Salisbury, C., & McGregor, G. (2005). Principals of inclusive schools. *National Institute for Urban School Improvement,* 1–12. Retrieved from http://glec.education.iupui.edu/equity/Principals_of_Inclusive_Schools.pdf.

Scruggs, T., & Mastropieri, M. (1996). Teacher perceptions of mainstreaming/inclusion, 1958–1995: A research synthesis. *Exceptional Children, 63*(1), 59–74.

Villa, R. A., & Thousand, J. S. (2005). *Creating an inclusive school* (2nd ed.). Alexandria, VA: ASCD.

Waldron, N., & McLeskey, J. (2010). Establishing a collaborative culture through comprehensive school reform. *Journal of Educational and Psychological Consultation, 20*(1), 58–74.

Wenger, E. (1998). Communities of practice: Learning as a social system. *Systems Thinker, 9*(5), 225–246.

Wenger, E. C., & Synder, W. M. (2000). Communities of practice: The organization frontier. *Harvard Business Review, 78*(6), 139–145.

SECTION III

Section III of this book is composed of a final chapter featuring frequently asked questions and corresponding answers and a final Voice of Inclusion.

In answering the 11 questions posed in Chapter 9, we tried to respectfully address concerns about inclusion by identifying underlying beliefs. Many unfounded stereotypes about people with disabilities have risen out of conventional "wisdom." Teachers who have never taught students with a particular disability might worry about behavioral issues that they only know about from incomplete media representations. Left unquestioned, such concerns can negatively influence our behavior as educators. We don't pretend to have definitive answers or a corner on what is politically correct. Our advice simply represents our collective best thinking at the time and is part of a dialogue that we hope will be ongoing and will include many voices in the future.

Concluding this book is the third and final Voice of Inclusion, "Everything About Bob Was Cool, Including His Cookies." This moving true story about the inclusion of a middle schooler with pervasive support needs illustrates how collaboration and creativity combined with many of the concepts and practices described in this book can result in school communities where each student truly belongs. The story reminds us that inclusion is more than a legal right or a set of strategies; it is about the opportunities we choose to provide—or deny—our youth.

CHAPTER 9

Questions, Concerns, Beliefs, and Practical Advice about Inclusive Education

Richard A. Villa, Jacqueline S. Thousand, Emma Van der Klift, John Udis, Ann I. Nevin, Norman Kunc, Paula Kluth, and James Chapple

There are no foolish questions and no man becomes a fool until he has stopped asking questions.

—Charles Steinmetz

Isn't general education inappropriate for some children? Are inclusion advocates suggesting that the federal law be changed and the "continuum of placement" model discarded?

A defining characteristic of an inclusive school is a "zero reject" (Lilly, 1971) philosophy. When we begin by identifying which groups of children cannot "make it," we miss the point: Peers of students who have been categorically excluded from general education might wonder, "If my school can exclude *them*, what would cause it to exclude *me*?" Educators and others have increasingly recognized that a solid sense of belonging is a prerequisite to quality in education (refer to the Circle of Courage in Chapter 2).

Teachers, and sometimes families, often make assumptions based on misperceptions of what students can and cannot achieve. Throughout history, people have assumed that various populations, such as those with cerebral palsy, autism, and deafness, were unable to learn (Crossley, 1997). Educators in the United States and elsewhere have also long held damaging negative assumptions about the learning potential of girls, students of color, and English language learners.

Inclusive education commits to every child and his or her different strengths and needs. Thus, a constellation of services *is taken to the child* rather than the child being *taken to the services.* We believe this makes more sense than a continuum-of-placement approach that removes children from the learning community. Ideally, an inclusive school provides supports within general education environments.

The issues of student placement and parent choice are closely linked. For some students with disabilities, the "regular" classroom may not be optimal, but it also may not be best for students *not* identified as disabled. Specifically, it is unlikely that every teacher whom a student encounters throughout his or her schooling will have all of the characteristics (e.g., content mastery, instructional skills, flexibility, warmth, compassion) that parents wish for their child. Although the dream is a perfect match every year, the reality is that most matches are only satisfactory. The nightmare, of course, is a very poor match.

As described in Chapters 4 and 7, the first step when planning for individual student differences is to identify the unique characteristics, skills, strategies, and knowledge that each student brings to different learning tasks and to identify likely educational mismatches. The next step is to determine how best to deliver the instruction, supports, and resources to remediate the mismatch and obtain desired outcomes. Fortunately, responses to individual student differences have mushroomed over the past decades due to increased competence and technology and the increasing presence of inclusive schools around the world. As educational experiences improve and continue to support *all* children, the concept of "continuum" becomes increasingly less relevant. Determinations about what constitutes a "least restrictive environment" will become moot as communities grow to embrace inclusion and segregated placements fall by the wayside.

There clearly are students for whom a traditional 12 years of 185 seven-hour school days does not constitute the magic formula for learning. Some children may benefit from experiences and relationships that typically do not exist within the walls of the school building (e.g., off-campus counseling groups for children who have experienced abuse) or employment training. Children who are experiencing emotional difficulties may temporarily need an altered "school day" that starts and ends on a flexible schedule and includes work and community service opportunities. Others may need a temporarily shortened day and a mentor relationship with a respected community member during periods of extreme stress. Still others may need yearlong support, including a summer program, to facilitate "staying out of trouble" in the community or to avoid a regression in learning.

Advocates of inclusion appear to be opposed to any type of homogeneous ability grouping. How are the needs of children identified as gifted and talented going to be met in inclusive general education classrooms? Those children are the leaders of tomorrow and shouldn't be held back in their learning or be expected to teach other children.

Advocates of inclusive education are not categorically against homogeneous grouping. They understand, however, that no two learners are the same and that grouping of any kind should be short-term and for specific, focused instruction. Educators are increasingly aware that intelligence is neither unitary nor fixed in time (see, for example, the discussion of Gardner's multiple intelligences theory in Chapter 7). Learning environments must be structured to nurture different types of intelligences. The *gifted and talented* label takes on a new meaning when thought of broadly (to include, for example, students who excel in gaming, art, auto mechanics, or interpersonal intelligence) rather than narrowly (i.e., defined by scoring well on a standardized test). A broader conceptualization of gifts and talents helps teachers to respect all learning styles and provide differentiated instruction, a range of activities, and various options for expressing knowledge.

Gifted and talented education (GATE), gifted and talented (GT), and talented and gifted (TAG) programs expressly celebrate and support the talents of *a few* and have perpetuated racial and socioeconomic segregation, as evidenced by the gross underrepresentation of children from ethnic minority groups and children living in poverty. By contrast, inclusive education acknowledges *everyone's* gifts and talents and helps all children reach their potential through the very educational experiences that were historically afforded only through GATE/GT/TAG programs: active, constructivist learning; opportunities for prolonged in-depth study of a special-interest area; opportunities for mentorships, internships, and other community experiences; and access to coursework in community colleges, businesses, and universities.

All students, including those considered for GATE/GT/TAG services, can greatly benefit from the instructional strategies used by inclusive educators to respond to student diversity. Specifically, peer-mediated teaching arrangements counter the lack of tolerance of others and the individualistic and competitive work styles that some students develop in GATE/GT/TAG programs. Further, when strategies are implemented well (i.e., with each student having individualized outcomes and tasks for contributing to a partnership effort), all students benefit by engaging in higher-order thinking skills as they plan how to effectively communicate ideas to their partners while simultaneously developing the interpersonal leadership skills necessary to succeed in the workplace.

Inclusive schooling does not mean that children with gifts and talents will not receive focused attention. On the contrary, capitalizing on the multiple intelligences theory, homogeneous groups could be arranged according to any number of criteria (e.g., musical preferences, recreational interests). In schools with an MTSS in place, homogeneous groups are deliberately structured to allow targeted instruction for some students and enrichment experiences (Slavin, 1987) for others as long as they can be shown to measurably reduce disparities in student understanding of the targeted skill or concept, teachers closely monitor student progress and make necessary adjustments to groups, and the type of instruction genuinely varies from one group to the next. Still, we strongly believe that students should spend most of their time at school in a heterogeneous peer group.

Are inclusion advocates primarily concerned with socialization? Aren't academics being sacrificed?

Academics, socialization, social/emotional development, life skills, employment skills, and recreation are just some of the areas of concern when planning for a child's individualized education program (IEP). No one area, including academics, should be ignored or viewed as the only potential priority area for a child's IEP. If we acknowledge that not every student must have the same objectives during an activity or lesson, any and all areas of concern can be addressed. Furthermore, as most state standards make clear, academics are important in large part because they enable children to become good communicators, reasoning problem-solvers, responsible global citizens, and nurturers of themselves and others. Long ago, educational futurists predicted that these characteristics would be pivotal for successfully negotiating the rapid changes of 21st century life (Benjamin, 1989).

It is unwise to inadvertently set up an "either/or" choice between academics and socialization. First, current best instructional practices and theories of learning such as constructivism teach us that learning is a constructed process that requires social interaction. Children seem to understand this. Secondly, socialization—cooperation, collaboration, and developing relationships—can boost academic learning. Students learning to speak, write, and read often do best when they are around other students who speak and who engage them in conversations throughout the day. Students learning to use and apply technology often acquire skills more quickly when other students can offer assistance and are available to play games, blog, e-mail, or cooperate on a web-based project.

In their study of students with significant disabilities, Kliewer and Biklen (2001) found that the social and complex nature of the inclusive classroom gives students critical opportunities to gain literacy skills. For example, Rebecca, a "primarily nonspeaking" 5th grader with autism, was considered "preliterate" by the professionals who evaluated her. Determined to include Rebecca in classroom life, her teacher had students brainstorm ways to include Rebecca throughout the day. Some girls thought of passing the kinds of notes to her that students typically pass to each other during class. Once students started passing notes to Rebecca, unfolding them for her, and then reading them to her, the teachers noted Rebecca's obvious interest and nodding responses (notes would say things like, "Do you like

James? Yes or no?"). As a result, Rebecca's team constructed a Yes/No response board and created a range of literacy experiences that were spin-offs of the initial note-passing experience (Kliewer & Biklen, 2001).

What is a child with severe disabilities going to do in a 9th grade science course?

This question really is asking why a student who has very different objectives from the majority of class members would be included in an activity or class that does not, at first glance, seem to meet his or her needs. Sometimes people don't realize just how rich a general education environment is, particularly for students with more pervasive and intense support needs. The variety of people, materials, and activities is endless and provides an ongoing flow of opportunities for communication and relationship building, incidental learning in areas not yet targeted as priority objectives, and direct instruction in a student's high-priority learning areas.

Creative thinking on the part of the student's support team is key to a student's meaningful participation in a general education environment. Teams always have at least four options:

1. Have the student do the *same* as everyone else (e.g., practice songs in music class);
2. Pursue *multilevel curriculum and instruction*, in which all students are working from the same curriculum but pursuing varied objectives at multiple levels according to their unique needs;
3. Employ *curriculum overlapping*, whereby students work on the same lesson but pursue objectives from different curricular areas (see the Voice of Inclusion following this chapter for examples); and
4. Offer *alternative activities* to allow for priority community or employment experiences, management needs (e.g., catheterization in the nurse's office), or when a general education activity cannot be adapted (e.g., mandatory statewide high-stakes testing).

We advise extreme caution when ruling an activity impossible to adapt or the general education classroom inappropriate for a student with intensive support needs. We have learned through experience that general education can meet the needs of most every child if adults and students collaborate and think creatively. Theory and practice exist to empower and equip educators to adapt instruction for any student.

How do we grade students with disabilities? Is it fair to give them an *A* or a *B* for doing work that is significantly different from the rest of the class or after we have provided them with accommodations and modifications to the curriculum and instruction?

The Every Student Succeeds Act (ESSA) of 2015 ensures that states and school districts track progress in the state curriculum for all students, including those with disabilities. So, nationwide, we have standards-based assessments of student performance that are unrelated to grading. Nevertheless, we recognize that grades are still the most common marks of performance in school and are highly valued by students, parents, and administrators (whose schools are evaluated partly on the basis of grades assigned). However, grading practices and procedures can be arbitrary and subjective. And, due to the inherent variability within and across schools in teacher grading *practices*, grades are not necessarily accurate demonstrations of what a child knows or can demonstrate. For example, within a particular school, an earned grade in one math class (e.g., calculus) may not mean the same as the same grade in another math class (e.g., general math). In fact, within the same *class*, two students receiving the same grade could have vastly divergent learning experiences. Before we engage in grading, we must first ask what its purpose is. Is it to compare one student's performance to another's, to a standard, or to the student's own past performance? There are more appropriate assessment methods for any of these.

Performance-based assessments are more compatible and supportive of children with and without disabilities than traditional standardized achievement testing. They also provide a much broader picture of what students actually can do and of the supports they need to perform successfully. As Nel Noddings has said, "We should move away from the question, Has Johnny learned X?" to the far more pertinent question, "What has Johnny learned?" (1992, p. 179).

Alternatives to traditional grading are available to teachers who want distinctions to appear on report cards and transcripts for students who have unique goals or who receive modifications; indeed, some teachers choose to use these alternatives for all of their students. The alternatives include pass/fail systems, student self-assessments, contracts with students, grading according to criteria or rubrics, portfolios, and technology-enabled assessment systems with incorporated scaffolding (Almond et al., 2010; Beech, 2005).

It should be noted that the Smarter Balanced and the Partnership for Assessment of Readiness for College and Careers (PARCC) assessment systems for measuring student performance on the Common Core State Standards employ digital technology and craft authentic assessment tasks (e.g., problem solving for "real" scenarios) that make assessment results more accurate. Digital technology allows assessment results to be more quickly gathered and processed, so that teachers can use the data sooner to differentiate instruction. (For information on assessment materials and projects funded by the U.S. Department of Education, see the OSEP Ideas That Work website at https://www.osepideasthatwork.org/federal-resources-stakeholders/tool-kitstool-kit-universal-design-learning-udl/letter.)

Another alternative is to use IEPs to determine grades. Students with disabilities have an advantage over other students in that they have an IEP that clearly defines objectives, any accommodations required during instruction and assessment, and criteria or a rubric for determining grades. Such clarification of expectations and success and grading criteria certainly would be of benefit to any student. IEPs are a federal requirement, and federal law requires educators to provide the accommodations identified in them.

Perhaps the questions we really should be asking are, "What student *wouldn't* benefit from differentiated assessment based on learning style, MI strengths, or differing interests?" or, "If we made accomodations for everyone and employed more of a portfolio approach where students' actual performances and products are presented, what would be the purpose of grading and report cards?" Should our focus be on whether students who are provided with accommodations should receive different grades, or on good teaching and differentiation to facilitate *all* children's learning?

Isn't inclusion in direct opposition to the national call for higher standards? Teachers are expected to prepare students to score well on tests. Won't the presence of children with disabilities negatively affect students' and schools' scores?

Inclusive education, ESSA, and Common Core standards all support conditions that lead to better instruction and learning, equality of opportunity to learn, and excellence in performance for all children.

Unfortunately, establishing standards and assessing through testing *alone* have not done much to equalize learning opportunities or significantly alter student outcomes. Kenneth Howe (1994) explains why:

> It strains credulity to suggest that implementing national standards and assessments could be anywhere near as effective a means of improving educational opportunity [or student outcomes] as addressing the conditions of schooling and society directly. It is rather like suggesting that the way to end world hunger is to first develop more rigorous standards of nutrition and then provide physicians with more precise means of measuring ratios of muscle-to-fat. (p. 31)

The 2015 ESSA authorization emphasizes flexibility in using effective, research-based assessment practices that support inclusion and allow children both with and without disabilities to thrive. Further, ESSA's emphasis on developing all students' literacy skills is important for students with disabilities, since literacy is the gateway skill for access to the rest of the general education curriculum (a stated goal of IDEIA).

There is no evidence to validate the concern that the presence of children with disabilities will negatively affect a district's norm-referenced achievement scores. In fact, studies have consistently indicated the contrary: When students with disabilities are provided with supports and services to learn in general education classrooms, not only do their peers maintain the same performance scores as before, but the students with disabilities experience higher academic and social achievement than previously.

The inclusion of students with disabilities in general education combined with research-based instructional practices should actually help teachers in standards-based classrooms. Students with and without disabilities need their teachers to learn and use the most effective instructional strategies, technology, educational materials, and assessment formats they can find. As discussed in Chapter 7, teachers can and do effectively use standards as a curricular guide while retaining multilevel, student-centered instruction and performance expectations.

Meeting standards is not the same as standardizing teaching or learning. In fact, standards can allow for different students in the same classroom to learn, practice, and show their accomplishments in different ways. For example, consider the following standard: "Explain to others how to solve a numerical problem." This standard can be met in various ways. Some students might use calculators or manipulatives to show their understanding, others might explain in writing, still others may express what they know by drawing diagrams or designing flow charts. There may be a range of complexity, too: some students might describe the process for adding single or double digits while others design and explain binomial equations.

How do we guarantee the physical and emotional safety of students in the same classroom with peers who have emotional or behavioral disabilities?

It is never possible to guarantee that every classroom, hallway, playground, lunchroom, and bus is completely safe. Violence is a societal problem, and permanent solutions to it will emerge only through community, interagency, and school collaboration. Still, solutions such as Schoolwide Positive Behavior Support (SWPBS) systems can help to make schools safer and more welcoming learning environments.

The best defenses against norm-violating behavior from students are effective instruction, motivating learning experiences, personalized accommodations, and SWPBS systems that spell out student behavioral expectations and recognize students who meet them. We need to wrap around a constellation of resources and services for students experiencing behavioral and emotional challenges, including but not limited to direct instruction of impulse-control, problem-solving, social, and anger-management skills; strategies for involving, empowering, and supporting students and their families; and intensive collaborations with outside agency personnel (for more, see Villa, Thousand, & Nevin, 2010).

We can bring this constellation of resources, supports, and services to the students rather than sending the students away or immersing them in separate programs. In fact, it is counterproductive to cluster students with emotional or behavioral issues in settings where they have limited access to prosocial models of behavior and are given the message that they do not belong with their peers. Meeting the complex psychological and educational needs of students with emotional and behavioral challenges is difficult. Matching intervention and support strategies to each student requires thoughtful consideration by teams of educators, parents, and students who care about and are committed to the student's success.

A basic responsibility of every school is to ensure freedom from physical harm for students and adults. No student has the right to harm another person. However, we know that students will sometimes place themselves and others in jeopardy. In anticipation of this, every school must have a well-articulated and understood crisis-management system that promotes student responsibility and choice at each stage of a crisis. Choices within a crisis management system might include

- allowing students to calm down in a predetermined alternative school setting;
- allowing students with parental permission to leave school grounds for a period of time;
- imposing in-school or out-of-school suspension for a short period of time, until a team can convene and identify the next steps;
- having a parent or mental-health, social-service, or police officer remove the student to a safe and supervised place; or
- allowing passive physical restraint by trained personnel.

Social, emotional, and behavioral struggles in schools are not just issues faced by students with disabilities. Many students experience bullying in today's schools, including those who are ethnically, linguistically, and racially diverse; dress or act outside the norms of the school; have different body types; and have learning differences. Educators are now asking new questions about the prevalence of teasing and bullying. Instead of asking, "Will this student be teased if he is in a regular classroom?" they should be asking, "How can we create school communities where all students feel safe, comfortable, and valuable?"

Schools must become communities where all students feel welcome and protected. If any student is scared or tormented at school, that student's placement should not be at risk. Instead, the school must change its practices and examine its culture. To prevent difficulties and promote safety, we need to establish proactive conflict resolution strategies such as teaching students how to resolve their own conflicts through peer mediation, how to use anger management to defuse dangerous situations, and how to stop bullying. National movements teaching children to be peacemakers (Johnson & Johnson, 2002; Villa et al., 2010) or effective members of cooperative learning groups help students to develop the skills they need to face controversy.

Inclusion would be nice, but it is unrealistic if not impossible given increasing student diversity, large class sizes, and decreased public funding. In some classes, 25 to 30 percent of the students are identified as disabled. This being the case, how can one teacher be expected to meet the needs of all students?

Given our cultural, racial, economic, and religious diversity, the idea that one educator working alone can successfully meet the disparate needs of all students seems outdated and impractical. A teacher working alone with traditional teaching methods (e.g., teacher-directed, predominantly independent or competitive student work structures with the same standard for all children) will likely be frustrated by student diversity.

A strikingly different organizational structure—co-teaching—is needed to address the heterogeneity of today's classrooms. As described in Chapter 6, co-teaching teams can involve any combination of classroom teachers, specialists, paraeducators, teacher candidates, community volunteers, and students themselves. Inclusive education shifts the role of the classroom teacher from "lone arranger" to "partner with supports." Collaborative organizational structures take advantage of the diverse experience, knowledge, and instructional approaches of various team members. In addition, the increased teacher-to-student ratio allows for more immediate and accurate diagnoses of student needs as well as more active student learning.

Often, the students themselves are overlooked as instructional and support resources. In inclusive classrooms, the teaching team invites students to partner in teaching arrangements (Villa et al., 2010). Students function as instructors, as advocates for themselves and peers, and as decision makers serving on school governance committees.

Do proponents of inclusive education advocate for eliminating special educators? How will children with disabilities have their unique needs met in a general education classroom without access to therapists and other trained personnel?

Inclusion proponents do *not* want to eliminate special educators or other specialists such as psychologists, physical and occupational therapists, and social workers from the learning environment. Indeed, inclusion *requires* the participation of professionals who are especially knowledgeable about human development and individual differences, particular reading or writing interventions, impulse-control techniques, mobility instruction, assistive technology, and augmentative and alternative communication.

The goal is always to ensure that every student receives needed supports and services. What inclusion proponents *do* call for is a change in the way that some specialists deliver expertise. Those who have worked alone with students away from the general education environment are being asked now to work together to address students' needs inside of it. This shift requires specialists to be willing to become models, coaches, and co-teachers so that they may pass on knowledge to others—teachers, parents, paraeducators, volunteers, and students.

Some children need regular, intensive, individualized instruction in order to acquire specific skills. How can the needs of children with disabilities be met if we cannot take children out of general education classrooms to supply them with this?

The expectation in an inclusive school is that any student can and should receive focused and intensive instruction as needed. The instruction may occur anywhere in the school that makes sense for the task rather than in an area to which only students with special needs are effectively "banished." Choosing who will deliver individualized instruction depends on any number of variables, from professional expertise to interest or personal relationship with the student. Students themselves have proven to be exceptional at delivering focused instruction and should not be forgotten as possible resources.

Meeting individualized learning needs requires us to change the nature of the general education classroom. When students are grouped heterogeneously and allowed to progress at their own pace without regard to age, grade, or level of ability or disability, individualization naturally occurs. Specialized instruction should be available to any child who may wish or need it, but should never be provided based only on a label attached to a child. As part of a comprehensive Multitiered System of Supports (MTSS), all students receive classroom-based instruction with individual or group interventions, as needed, based on data analysis and progress monitoring of student performance (see Chapter 5).

Schools that embrace the belief that learning can occur in many ways and in many different places have no trouble creatively designing ways to individualize and differentiate instruction. The false assumption exists that the only children who could benefit from learning life skills are those eligible for special education, when *all* children need life skills instruction in a curriculum component.

Won't children with disabilities be teased and ridiculed by the other children without disabilities?

The unfortunate reality is that children do face ridicule, teasing, and rejection in school. People are teased for many reasons (e.g., differences in perceived abilities, physical characteristics, ethnic background, sexual orientation, religion, language, culture, socioeconomic status). Sometimes, teasing is only a misguided attempt to express liking someone or to build personal connections. We do not believe that the solution to the problem of teasing is the removal of anyone who is different from the general education environment.

Teachers cannot eliminate teasing and ridicule among children altogether, but they can promote a caring ethic in their classes through, for example, meetings during which students determine ways to be more supportive of one another. Teachers may also reduce incidents of teasing by teaching children the reasons for it and the unfortunate results that it can have and by using learning structures that require positive treatment of classmates (e.g., cooperative learning groups). Presenting students with activities designed to stir their concerns for social justice can be an effective way to build their support for students with disabilities. Having students plan for transitions into the classroom and welcome students with disabilities can also have positive effects.

At the heart of the solution to teasing is teacher and administrator modeling. Students observe, reflect on, and imitate adult behavior toward people who are different and the problem-solving strategies adults use to deal with teasing and discrimination.

Experience leads us to believe that less ridicule occurs in inclusive schools—perhaps because they offer more explicit teaching on how to mediate conflict (see, for example, Villa et al., 2010). Children who begin their educational careers in the same classrooms as children with disabilities seem comfortable with and accepting of difference.

References

Almond, P., Winter, P., Cameto, R., Russell, M., Sato, E., Clarke-Midura, J., & Lazarus, S. (2010). Technology-enabled and universally designed assessment: Considering access in measuring the achievement of students with disabilities: A foundation for research. *Journal of Technology, Learning, and Assessment, 10*(5). Retrieved from http://ejournals.bc.edu/ojs/index.php/jtla/article/view/1605/1453.

Benjamin, S. (1989). An ideascape for education. What futurists recommend. *Educational Leadership, 47*(1), 8–14.

Crossley, R. (1997). *Speechless: Facilitating communication for people without voices.* New York: Dutton.

Every Student Succeeds Act of 2015. The 2015 reauthorization of the Elementary and Secondary Education Act (HB1). Retrieved from https://www.congress.gov/bill/114th-congress/senate-bill/1177/text.

Gardner, H. (1993). *Multiple intelligences: The theory in practice.* New York: Basic Books.

Gardner, H. (2011). *Frames of mind: The theory of multiple intelligences* (3rd ed.). New York: Basic Books.

Howe, K. (1994). Standards, assessment, and equality of educational opportunity. *Educational Researcher, 23*(8), 27–32.

Johnson, R. T. & Johnson, D. W. (2002). Teaching students to be peacemakers: A meta-analysis. *Journal of Research in Education, 12*(1), 25–39.

Kliewer, C., & Biklen, D. (2001). "School's not really a place for reading": A research synthesis of the literate lives of students with severe disabilities. *The Journal of the Association for Persons with Severe Handicaps, 26*(1), 1–12.

Lilly, M.S. (1971). A training-based model for special education. *Exceptional Children, 37*(10), 745–749.

Noddings, N. (1992). *The challenge to care in schools.* New York: Teachers College Press.

Slavin, R. (1987). Ability grouping and achievement in elementary school: A best-evidence synthesis. *Review of Educational Research, 57*(3), 293–336.

Villa, R. A., Thousand, J. S., & Nevin, A. (2010). *Collaborating with students in instruction and decision making: The untapped resource.* Thousand Oaks, CA: Corwin.

VOICE OF INCLUSION

Everything About Bob Was Cool, Including His Cookies

Richard A. Villa

"Dr. Villa, I made Bob a promise. Now I know I won't be able to keep it. I feel really bad. I don't know if I can—or should—tell you about it," a student named Bubba said to me.

Who is Bubba? Who is Bob? What was the promise, and why couldn't Bubba keep it?

Bob Comes to Winooski

I first heard about Bob when Totyona, a former paraeducator in the Winooski (Vermont) School District, called to ask if her new foster son, Bob, could go to school in Winooski. Because Totyona and her husband, Todd, both resided in Winooski, my answer, of course, was yes.

Totyona then gave me more information. Bob was a young man with multiple disabilities, including cerebral palsy. For the previous 14 years, he had lived with his mom and dad in a small town in northeastern Vermont. He had attended a special education class where Totyona had been one of the educators. In May of that year, Bob's mom became seriously ill and was no longer able to care for him, so Bob went to live in a residential medical and educational facility. His initial stay was to be six weeks, but by the time Totyona called me, Bob had lived there for six months. With his mom still unable to care for him, his stay had been extended.

Although Bob did not, at the time, communicate orally or through sign language or a communication device, I believe he clearly communicated his sense of loss while in the residential facility. He shed 16 pounds—a significant weight loss for someone as thin and medically fragile as Bob.

Bob was the first student with intensive support needs to be included into general education middle-level classrooms at Winooski. A great deal of time, energy, and planning went into his transition. Bob's natural parents and foster mother were very much a part of the transition planning. A Winooski education team comprising a middle-level science teacher, a special educator, a speech and language pathologist, a school nurse, and myself—the special education administrator—visited the facility where Bob was staying and videotaped him so that those who could not visit could "meet" him before he arrived. We met with everyone who provided services for Bob. We then detailed a plan for his transition. Our goal was for Bob to attend school full-time within six weeks.

In retrospect, one of the most important transition activities was the immediate involvement of students. A special educator who became Bob's service coordinator and I visited every middle-level classroom and "introduced" Bob to the students. We showed video clips of Bob and described what we knew about him, including his strengths and some of his needs. Even though we didn't know a great deal about him, we pretended to know even less. We asked the students to help us brainstorm strategies and resources to support Bob in his new school.

The students were great! Their advice ranged from the kinds of music and notebooks Bob should have so that he'd "fit in" to where he should hang out to be "cool." (At the time, if you were a middle-level student, the cool place to hang out was by the bike racks before school.) Students asked many questions, including how we intended to grade Bob. It was clear to them that we would need to make some adaptations.

Laura, a middle-level student who happened to be the daughter of the superintendent, was one of the students who greatly anticipated Bob's arrival. I learned in a conversation with the superintendent that he had overheard his daughter speak to her friends about Bob's impending presence with such excitement that he had thought Bob was some sort of teen idol. Even though Bob had not yet been to the school, he was one of the most "popular" students. Everyone had the opportunity to plan for him and to get to know about him; everyone was talking about him and wanting to meet him in person.

Today, a visitor to the school would not be surprised to see a student with intensive support needs as a natural part of our student body. But at that time, Bob was "different"—at least initially.

Building Bob's Supports

The team of adults who assembled to work with Bob after his arrival put an extraordinary amount of time and energy into the planning process. In the beginning, we seemed to have more questions than answers. We secured technical assistance from state and local resources, such as the statewide Interdisciplinary Team for Students with Intensive Needs (Vermont I-Team). Having Totyona, Bob's foster mother, as a member of Bob's core team was extremely valuable. As a former teacher of and now a parent to Bob, she brought with her a dual perspective and a wealth of information, concerns, and ideas.

To respond to Bob's needs, both adults and students assumed new roles. For example, the speech and language pathologist found herself among those helping Bob to eat at lunchtime. That role change allowed her to assess Bob's oral-motor skills, work with him on communication issues, and establish a relationship. By the same token, some professional and paraprofessional staff members received training in handling and positioning techniques and range-of-motion activities.

In their new roles, students were recruited as natural peer supports and tutors to assist in Bob's education program and actively involve him in class experiences. A dozen or so classmates became his peer-support network outside of school. As Bob's peer tutors, peer buddies, and circle of friends, they helped include Bob in nonacademic aspects of school (e.g., by meeting him at the bus, getting him from class to class, encouraging and facilitating his attendance at after-school activities) and in after-school and weekend events. Bob's network was very diverse: There were students who were very popular, students who were quiet, students who had the full range of academic talent or achievement, and students who had siblings with disabilities. They were possibly the most diverse crew of kids you could imagine. They had lots of different interests, but all shared one in common: a concern for Bob.

Initially, Bob's Individualized Education Program (IEP) team targeted three priority goal areas. Communication was the highest priority; the team had goals for Bob to increase his vocalizations and visual tracking abilities, reliably distinguish among things important in his environment, respond to his name, explore ways for him to indicate choice, and establish his use of a panel switch to activate assistive communication and other devices. A second goal area was socialization: Bob's team wanted him to be part of many social activities, to spontaneously interact with peers, and to develop relationships. Bob's health was a third priority: specifically, gaining back the 16 pounds he had lost and maintaining or regaining his range of motion. All of these goals were met during Bob's first year as a Winooski student.

Year 1: Snapshots of Bob's School Life

To meet Bob's goals, his team used a systematic IEP goal/general education matrix procedure (see Janney & Snell, 2013; Udvari-Solner, 1995) to examine the possible times, places, classes, and activities within the general education schedule during which Bob's goals might be directly or indirectly addressed. The team then developed a schedule. In Bob's first year, the schedule included teacher advisory, science, math, social studies, physical education, library, technology education, and computer classes.

Teacher Advisory

During the morning teacher advisory period, Bob would frequently work with classmates by using his panel switch device. If Bob hit the panel switch, music would begin to play. The music was always chosen by Bob and the students with whom he was working. They encouraged Bob to use the panel switch, and when he did, their efforts were rewarded by the music they selected.

Science

As a former middle-level science teacher, I took great interest in observing what went on in Bob's science class. I discovered that, in many ways, some things never change. For example, one day the class was engaged in dissecting frogs. Some students really got involved in the activity, some found it "gross," and some took parts of the frog and wiggled them in front of other kids' faces, eliciting giggles and screams.

I was fascinated by Bob's participation. Students were working in cooperative learning groups of three at lab tables. Each group had a dissecting pan with a frog in it and dissecting tools. I noticed that Bob's lab group had the frog in the dissecting pan, but that the group hadn't placed the pan on the table as the other groups had. Instead, the pan sat on the lap tray connected to Bob's wheelchair, and Bob's teammates were gathered around it doing their work.

A couple of other objects also sat on the lap tray, including the blue cup that Bob used to drink water and juice. During the course of the activity, Bob's teammates would occasionally ask questions such as "Bob, do you want a drink?" or "Bob, can you look at the blue cup?" Bob's responses to questions were recorded by a paraeducator who was seated off to the side, not directly involved in the activity but available, when needed, to support Bob or any other student in the class. The students were well aware of Bob's object-discrimination and choice-making goals, and they easily incorporated them into the dissection activity. Another goal, increased vocalizations, was also realized: Bob laughed and squealed as readily as any student when a teammate held up a part of the frog and wiggled it in his face. Students aptly involved Bob in planned activities, enabling him to address his objectives while simultaneously working on their own.

Math

Bob also participated in math class. (Recall that visual tracking was one of his communication goals—we wanted him to increase his ability to track movement with his eyes.) The math teacher had a booming voice and paced around the room. We found that by positioning Bob in such a way that he could see the teacher, Bob's eyes could easily track him. We even began to see his head move. The teacher used Bob's and other students' names in word problems as he started each class. For example, after the class had studied the radius, diameter, and circumference of a circle, he asked, "Given the radius of the tires on Bob's wheelchair and the distance from this room to the cafeteria, how many revolutions would it take to get Bob from here to the lunchroom?" The students measured, computed, and checked their answers by wheeling Bob to the cafeteria. Activities like this allowed us to assess when Bob recognized his name and allowed Bob to be a meaningful part of the classroom community.

Social Studies

Bob's social studies teacher typically began class with an activity that involved students coming to the front of the room and briefly presenting newsworthy happenings. Though they were encouraged to report about events in Vermont, they were free to report about national, world, or personal events.

I observed the class on Bob's day to report the news. Bob and his speech and language pathologist, Tracy, came to the front of the room to explain how a new communication system for Bob worked. Bob and his team wanted everyone to know how to use it. Tracy secured a large sheet of Plexiglass to Bob's lap tray that had a symbol for "yes" in the upper right and a symbol for "no" in the upper left. Tracy then asked Bob several questions, asking that he respond by looking at the symbol that indicated his preference. Using his eyes, Bob then answered some great questions from his classmates. In the same amount of time it took for any student to deliver the news, Bob's classmates learned how to use this new system and now were equipped to "talk with" Bob. From my observation of his classmates' body language and enthusiastic questioning, the students were vastly more interested in Bob's presentation than in all the others. It was an exciting moment, as Bob now had his first "voice" with which to communicate with his friends, classmates, teachers, and family.[1]

Physical Education

Bob's adaptive physical education took place in the gym and on the playing fields with the other students. If you visited Bob's gym class, you'd see him being repositioned and doing range-of-motion exercises on a floor mat. During a wrestling unit, Bob was joined on the floor by a lot of other students. During baseball season, he went outside on the baseball field whenever his classmates were out. Bob was a designated base runner for his team. When his batting partner hit a ball, Bob was wheeled quickly around the bases. I can still hear him laughing as he went from first base to second, to third, and home.

Year 2: Entrepreneurship and Social Life

By the start of Bob's second year at school, 8th grade, his family and support team began to ask questions about what was going to happen to him after high school and, consequently, added employment and vocationally oriented goals to his IEP.

Budding Entrepreneurs

After some brainstorming, Bob's team came up with the idea of helping him form a small cookie business with three other classmates who had an interest in entrepreneurship. The business became known as Cota's Cool Cookies—"Cota" because that was Bob's last name and "Cool" because the "secret" ingredient was cool mints. Bob was the chief executive officer and head chef. By using his panel switch, he could turn on an electric beater that mixed the cookie batter. The other students in the business baked, packaged, and distributed the cookies.

[1] The assistive technology and augmentative communication devices, applications (apps), and other high tech electronic tools available today for students to use to assist in their communication were not available when Bob attended Winooski in the 1980s. Today, the "yes/no" communication board that Bob used may seem terribly low tech and limiting. In its day, however, it was innovative and a powerful first step in giving Bob a voice.

Cota's Cool Cookies was a collaborative enterprise that involved many other students in the school. Students with an interest in business set up contracts and maintained the books. Students in the art classes participated in a contest to design the product label. Cota's Cool Cookies were sold in the district's schools and in two neighboring school districts during lunch. They were also sold at the National Guard Armory, Winooski City Hall, and many other places in the community. Despite the numerous supplies that they'd had to purchase, Bob and his business partners turned a profit within a couple of months.

Life Outside of School

Bob's involvement with his peers extended beyond the school day. I remember his foster mother saying, "I used to think it would be great if Bob had some friends coming over after school. Well, they came, and do you have any idea what it is like to have half a dozen middle-school-aged kids in your house all day?"

I will never forget the time a teacher said to me, "I think Bob's going to be in a fight." I found that quite interesting and asked her to explain.

"You see," she said, "Bob has been invited to the Halloween dance by a cheerleader, and her ex-boyfriend, who is on the football team, is not too happy. He says he's going to pound Bob's face. What are we going to do?"

We decided to do what we would do for any other student. We monitored the situation and followed the policy of not intervening unless absolutely necessary. After all, changing boyfriends and girlfriends is a part of normal adolescent development. Bob didn't get into a fight with the football player, and he ended up at the dance—dressed as Beetlejuice and doing wheelies on the dance floor.

Transitions

Toward the end of Bob's 8th grade year, Totyona notified the school that Bob would be moving with his foster family to a neighboring town and new school district. The members of his support and friendship circle were saddened by the news, as were the teachers, and the principal, and so was I.

Before Bob came to Winooski, everyone wondered how he was going to fit in. Would he be accepted and appreciated for his individuality? I remember a teacher wondering, "Is he just going to sit in the back of my room, drooling, making noises, and disrupting my class?" Then he got to know Bob. Six months later, that same teacher said, "He has had such a powerfully positive influence on the students in my class. Can he please stay another year?" I reminded the teacher of our school's adherence to the principle of age-appropriate placement. Bob needed to move along the grades with his peers.

Students in Bob's peer support circle demonstrated their knowledge of the importance of transition planning. Several classmates approached the administrators and requested to go to the school that Bob would be attending in the fall so they could facilitate his smooth transition. They wanted to be sure both students and staff knew what Bob could do and how they could support him. We contacted Bob's new school in late May, and the special educator responsible for his program promised to get back to us. After summer break, some students were asked to come and speak with Bob's new classmates and teachers. In October, three students went, and the effect of their words and advocacy for their friend was evidenced in the thank-you letter from Bob's new school:

> Moriah Gosselin and Jason Messick spoke with Bob's afternoon classes. They spoke articulately and with humor and covered many important aspects of Bob's inclusion at your school. Most important was the regard and fondness for Bob evident in their presentations. They were excellent.
>
> Chandra Duba, who came to school at 7 a.m. to speak with Bob's morning classes, discussed not only Bob's experiences at Winooski, but also her own experiences with her siblings with disabilities.
>
> Although Bob was the focus of their work, the effect of those young people went far beyond Bob. The attitudes and behaviors they modeled were lessons for us all about friendship and mutual respect. What they taught us made the way easier here for many students with disabilities. (K. Lewis, personal communication, November 20, 1989)

Loss

Early in December, Winooski students went back to see how Bob was doing. They excitedly reported that Bob looked great, seemed happy, and had a whole new peer support network. That Saturday, I spoke with Bob's foster parents. They were happy with Bob's transition and his emerging new support group.

On Sunday of the same weekend, while sitting at the breakfast table with his foster family, Bob suddenly died. He had contracted an undetected pneumonia that was too much for his fragile system to handle.

On Monday, I delivered the news. In all my years in education, the hardest thing I have had to do was gather Bob's Winooski classmates and tell them that their friend had died. Many students wanted to go to Bob's funeral, so the school arranged for a bus to take staff members and students on the two-hour trip to pay their last respects.

As I sat in that funeral parlor and looked around, any doubts that I might have had about the benefits of inclusive education disappeared forever. I recalled funerals that I had attended for other students who had died—students who had been educated apart from their neighborhood peers. Those funerals usually were attended only by the family and other adults. It seemed to me that, in many ways, their lives had been anonymous. By contrast, this room was filled with children—a diverse group of Bob's peers who now were mourning the loss of a friend. Bob had not lived an anonymous life. He had died with dignity, respect, and friendship.

After the funeral, the bus ride home was silent. Then, little by little, students began to tell stories, amusing anecdotes, and remembrances about Bob. One student recalled playing a joke on a substitute teacher when he turned his back by taking Bob in his wheelchair and disappearing. Another student recalled the superintendent expressing concern about liability because Bob was being wheeled so quickly around the baseball diamond. They said that they didn't care if they had gotten into trouble with the superintendent; just hearing Bob laugh as he rounded the bases was worth the risk.

Staff members recalled how much planning had gone into Bob's initial transition into Winooski and how much they had learned from the experience that subsequently benefited other students. We discussed how much we had known intuitively about how to meet Bob's needs. We reflected on how Bob's presence taught students and adults alike to appreciate the differences in others and themselves. We talked about the future. What if one of Bob's classmates became the parent of a child with a significant disability? Would having known Bob and his zest in life make a difference for that parent? Bob's classmates are the employers of the future. When approached with the prospect of hiring somebody like Bob, they might recall all that Bob was capable of doing and choose to employ that person.

It was on the bus that Bubba, a star football, baseball, and hockey player, approached me with his dilemma. I encouraged him to say what was on his mind, and he finally did. As it turns out, Bubba had promised Bob that when the two of them turned 21, they were going to go out and get rip-roaring drunk together. Clearly, drinking isn't what we want students to be thinking about, but the fact is that many do anticipate "becoming legal." For me, Bubba's confession was symbolic of a fundamental goal of inclusive schooling. You see, Bubba did not see Bob as a person with a disability. Bubba saw Bob as Bob—a friend. What Bubba dreamed about for the two of them was no different from what he and other teens dream and scheme about, and Bob was part of it all.

Guidance personnel supported Bob's peers in finding ways to express their grief. Some students wrote in journals, others spoke with counselors, and others collected money to donate in Bob's name and memory. Some students expressed anger and frustration at anyone who prevented a student like Bob from attending their school.

Advocacy Lives On

Shortly after Bob's death, a unique opportunity for advocacy came along that helped some students deal with their emotions. I had become aware of a girl in Canada, Becky Till, who was 14 years old, as was Bob. Like Bob, she had cerebral palsy and lived with a foster family. Becky's foster parents wanted her to attend their community's local school, but despite four years of advocacy efforts, they had yet to win her access. We made Winooski students aware of this opportunity for advocacy, and several of them subsequently wrote to the Ontario Ministry of Education and the school board of Becky's town, explaining why she belonged in school.

To mount further pressure, Becky's mother put on a conference in New Market, Ontario. She invited me and other disability rights advocates to speak. Although my words might have been helpful, I knew it would be more important for the audience to hear from students. Two of Bob's friends, Bubba and Moriah, traveled to Ontario and articulated their own and their classmates' views as to why Bob and Becky belonged in school. When asked why, they responded simply, "Because they're human." They spoke of the benefits of all students being educated together. Bubba expressed, emotionally, "Nothing hurts more than losing someone you love." The students' message was strong and moving, as reflected in the Sunday *Toronto Sun* headline: "Bubba Tells Becky, Fight Until You Win!"

Bob's Legacy and Lessons

It has been nearly three decades since Bob's death, but in his short time on earth, he touched my life and the lives of others in a profound way that continues to live on. He demonstrated for us the value of collaboration, inclusive education, friendship, and saying "yes" to the unknown. He is fondly remembered.

Everything about Bob was cool, including his cookies.

References

Janney, R., & Snell, M. E. (2013). *Teachers' guides to inclusive practices: Modifying schoolwork.* Baltimore: Paul H. Brookes.

Udvari-Solner, A. (1995). A process for adapting curriculum in inclusive classrooms. In R. A. Villa & J. S. Thousand (Eds.), *Creating an inclusive school.* Alexandria, VA: ASCD.

Villa, R. A., Thousand, J. S., & Nevin, A. I. (2010). *Collaborating with students in instruction and decision making: The untapped resource.* Thousand Oaks, CA: Corwin.

INDEX

Note: The letter *f* following a page number denotes a figure.

About the Editors and Contributors

Editors

Richard A. Villa is President of Bayridge Consortium, Inc. His primary field of expertise is the development of administrative and instructional support systems for educating all students within general education settings. Rich is recognized as an educational leader who motivates and works collaboratively with others to implement current and emerging exemplary educational practices. He has been a classroom teacher, special education administrator, pupil personnel services director, and director of instructional services, and has authored 19 books and more than 120 articles and chapters. Known for his enthusiastic, humorous style, Rich has presented at international, national, and state educational conferences and has provided technical assistance to departments of education in the United States, Canada, Vietnam, Jamaica, Scotland, and Honduras and to university personnel, public school systems, and parent and advocacy organizations. Additional information about Villa can be found on his website: ravillabayridge.com.

Jacqueline S. Thousand is Professor Emerita in the College of Education, Health, and Human Services of California State University San Marcos, where she designed and coordinated the School of Education's special education professional preparation and master's programs. She previously directed the Inclusion Facilitator and Early Childhood/Special Education graduate and postgraduate programs at the University of Vermont, and coordinated federal grants concerned with the inclusion of students with disabilities in local schools. A nationally known teacher, author, systems change consultant, and disability rights and inclusive education advocate, she is the author of numerous books, research articles, and chapters on issues related to inclusive schooling, organizational change strategies, differentiated instruction and universal design, co-teaching and teaming, cooperative group learning, creative problem solving, and positive behavioral supports. She is actively involved in international teacher education and inclusive education endeavors and serves on the editorial boards of several national and international journals.

Contributors

James W. Chapple, EdD, educational consultant, 1230 Cherokee Path, Vermilion, OH 44089. E-mail: chappjw@aol.com.

Mary Falvey, PhD, Emeriti Professor, Division of Special Education and Counseling, California State University, Los Angeles, CA 90601. E-mail: mafalvey525@cs.com.

Christine C. Givner, PhD, Dean and Professor, College of Education, State University of New York at Fredonia, NY 14063. E-mail: christine.givner@fredonia.edu.

Paula Kluth, PhD, independent scholar and education consultant and Adjunct Professor of Education, National-Louis University, 4539 N. Lowell Ave., Chicago, IL 60630. E-mail: pkluth@earthlink.net.

Norman Kunc, Co-Director, The Broadreach Centre, New Westminster, British Columbia, Canada V3M 5V4. E-mail: nkunc@telus.net.

Ann Nevin, PhD, Professor Emerita, Arizona State University, Tempe, AZ 34205 E-mail: ann.nevin@asu.edu.

Jonathan Udis, Director, Vermont Schoolhouse Seminars, 46 East Hill, Middlesex, VT 05602. E-mail: jon@vermontschoolhouse.com.

Alice Udvari-Solner, PhD, University of Wisconsin–Madison, Department of Curriculum and Instruction, 225 N. Mills St., Madison, WI 53706. E-mail alice@education.wisc.edu.

Emma Van der Klift, Co-Director, The Broadreach Centre, New Westminster, British Columbia, Canada V3M 5V4. E-mail: emmavdk@telus.net.

Joe Vargo, 241 Dorchester Avenue, Syracuse, NY 13203. E-mail: joev@macny.org.

Rosalind Vargo, 241 Dorchester Avenue, Syracuse, NY 13203. E-mail: RoV@twcny.rr.com.

Yazmin Pineda Zapata, EdD, Program Manager/Inclusion Specialist, Health Sciences High and Middle College, 3910 University Ave., Suite 100, San Diego, CA 92105. E-mail: ypineda@hshmc.org.

Related Resources

At the time of publication, the following ASCD resources were available (ASCD stock numbers appear in parentheses). For up-to-date information about ASCD resources, go to www.ascd.org. You can search the complete archives of Educational Leadership at http://www.ascd.org/el.

ASCD Edge Group

Exchange ideas and connect with other educators interested in inclusion on the social networking site ASCDEdge® at http://ascdedge.ascd.org/.

Print Products

Educational Leadership: Resilience and Learning (September 2013) (#114018)

Inclusive Schools in Action: Making Differences Ordinary by James McLeskey and Nancy L. Waldron (#100210)

Teaching in Tandem: Effective Co-Teaching in the Inclusive Classroom by Gloria Lodato Wilson and Joan Blednick (#110029)

Co-Planning for Co-Teaching: Time-Saving Routines That Work in Inclusive Classrooms (ASCD Arias) by Gloria Lodato Wilson (#SF117018)

A Principal's Guide to Special Education, 3rd Edition by David F. Bateman and C. Fred Bateman (#315052)

A Teacher's Guide to Special Education by David F. Bateman and Jennifer L. Cline (#116019)

For more information, send an e-mail to member@ascd.org; call 1-800-933-2723 or 703-578-9600, press 2; send a fax to 703-575-5400; or write to Information Services, ASCD, 1703 N. Beauregard St., Alexandria, VA 22311-1714 USA.